Praise for *Succeeding with SOA*

"Like so many acronyms in public currency, SO   ent things to different people. Paul Brown deftly in the trap of overstating the case for SOA. Instea   ...e topic skillfully into focus, zeroing in on the concepts u...u. must be understood in order to be effective. Paul's purpose, as I've found so often in his presentations and conversations, is to get to the core of real-world architectural issues that make the difference between success and failure. Paul doesn't sit in an ivory tower pontificating; he gets right down to the critical issues in order to develop effective real-life strategies."

—From the Foreword by Jonathan Mack,
Senior Technical Architect, Guardian Life Insurance Company

"As Paul Brown explains in this fine book, there is more to software development than just writing code. Successful software requires deep thought and strategy. It requires the coordination and marshalling of the resources and intellect of the entire company, both business and IT. I learned much from reading his manuscript and heartily endorse the finished book."

—Dr. Michael Blaha,
author and industrial consultant

"Paul Brown has provided a practical and actionable guide that will illuminate the way for Business and IT Leaders involved in IT strategy, planning, architecture, and project management. A successful adoption of SOA will touch every aspect of the business and change the way IT does business. This book does a good job of describing the organizational challenges and risks and providing suggestions to manage them. It also dives deeply into the architectural techniques that can be employed in order to align the service architecture with the business, thus providing maximum benefit and continued funding for your SOA transformation."

—Maja Tibbling,
Lead Enterprise Architect, Con-way Enterprise Services

"*Succeeding with SOA* achieves where most books on service-oriented architectures fail. It accurately describes what practitioners are seeing, as well as why, and gives them practical examples through case studies and instruction. Most useful both for those about to take the plunge and those who are already soaking."

—Charly Paelinck,
Vice President, Development and Architecture, Harrah's Entertainment

"This book is a must-read for architects and SOA practitioners. It provides an important foundation for a SOA strategy. Brown emphasizes the importance of aligning services with their business processes, building capabilities using strong enterprise architecture standards, and ensuring an effective governance process. The book promotes the notion of mutual dependency between managing a business using business processes and managing its IT with SOA. By aligning the two paradigms, a business can become more agile, able to adapt to change both quickly and economically. This is the promise of SOA."

—Sunny Tara,
Director, IT, Enterprise Architecture and Services, Harrah's Entertainment

Succeeding with SOA

Succeeding with SOA

Realizing Business Value
Through Total Architecture

Paul C. Brown

✦ Addison-Wesley

Upper Saddle River, NJ • Boston • Indianapolis • San Francisco
New York • Toronto • Montreal • London • Munich • Paris • Madrid
Capetown • Sydney • Tokyo • Singapore • Mexico City

Many of the designations used by manufacturers and sellers to distinguish their products are claimed as trademarks. Where those designations appear in this book, and the publisher was aware of a trademark claim, the designations have been printed with initial capital letters or in all capitals.

The author and publisher have taken care in the preparation of this book, but make no expressed or implied warranty of any kind and assume no responsibility for errors or omissions. No liability is assumed for incidental or consequential damages in connection with or arising out of the use of the information or programs contained herein.

The publisher offers excellent discounts on this book when ordered in quantity for bulk purchases or special sales, which may include electronic versions and/or custom covers and content particular to your business, training goals, marketing focus, and branding interests. For more information, please contact:

U.S. Corporate and Government Sales
(800) 382-3419
corpsales@pearsontechgroup.com

For sales outside the United States please contact:

International Sales
international@pearsoned.com

This Book Is Safari Enabled

The Safari® Enabled icon on the cover of your favorite technology book means the book is available through Safari Bookshelf. When you buy this book, you get free access to the online edition for 45 days.

Safari Bookshelf is an electronic reference library that lets you easily search thousands of technical books, find code samples, download chapters, and access technical information whenever and wherever you need it.

To gain 45-day Safari Enabled access to this book:

- Go to http://www.awprofessional.com/safarienabled
- Complete the brief registration form
- Enter the coupon code ALIZ-IBMH-RTB8-ESH9-VWZ9

If you have difficulty registering on Safari Bookshelf or accessing the online edition, please e-mail customer-service @safaribooksonline.com.

Visit us on the Web: www.awprofessional.com

Library of Congress Cataloging-in-Publication Data

Brown, Paul C.
   Succeeding with SOA : realizing business value through total architecture / Paul C. Brown.
       p. cm.
   Includes index.
   ISBN-13: 978-0-321-50891-1 (pbk. : alk. paper)
   ISBN-10: 0-321-50891-2
   1. Computer architecture. 2. Computer network architectures. 3. Business enterprises—Computer networks—Management. I. Title.
   QA76.9.A73B83 2007
   004.2'2—dc22
                                                                        2007007415

ISBN 13:   978-0-321-50891-1
ISBN 10:   0-321-50891-2
Text printed in the United States on recycled paper at Courier in Stoughton, Massachusetts.
2nd printing   July 2007

In memory of Professor William Cady Stone

———

A lifetime committed to sharing the light of understanding

Contents

Figures

Tables

Foreword

When Guardian Life Insurance recently asked me to select someone who could provide an architectural overview to guide one of our most transformative reengineering projects, my response was instantaneous: Dr. Paul Brown. We needed someone who could relate high-level SOA concepts to down-to-earth, battle-tried experience, someone who could distinguish insight from hype. Paul did not disappoint: The principles Paul enumerated and practical solutions he offered continue to help direct our enterprise's evolution.

Now Paul brings his expertise to the broader public in this insightful and thought-provoking book. Like so many acronyms in public currency, SOA means many different things to different people. Paul deftly avoids getting caught in the trap of overstating the case for SOA. Instead, he brings the topic skillfully into focus, zeroing in on the concepts that must be understood in order to be effective. Paul's purpose, as I've found so often in his presentations and conversations, is to get to the core of real-world architectural issues that make the difference between success and failure. Paul doesn't sit in an ivory tower pontificating; he gets right down to the critical issues in order to develop effective real-life strategies.

From the days when I was coauthoring the canonical XML model for the human resources industry to more recent experiences such as leading Enterprise Architecture at 1800Flowers.com, I've faced innumerable challenges that Paul's work illuminates with acute clarity. Paul knows, as do any of us who've tried to make SOA work, that real environments aren't ideal realms where everything fits neatly and one size fits all. If they were, we wouldn't need Paul's insights into SOA as much as we do.

This spring I'm giving a keynote address on SOA at the *Transformation and Innovation Conference* in Washington, DC. Other keynoters are CIOs and CTOs of government agencies, including NASA and the Departments of Commerce and Defense, with budgets in excess of a billion dollars. In the audience, there will be those at the other end of the spectrum—individuals charged with building a SOA from scratch with minimal resources. In preparing for my presentation, I couldn't think of a better source than Paul Brown. This book should be required reading for the loftiest executive—IT or business—down to the rawest newbie. Paul's clear and impartial analysis cuts through the jargon to the core of what needs to be understood about SOA to be successful.

Jonathan Mack
Senior Technical Architect
Guardian Life Insurance Company
March 2007

Preface

Are you worried about getting a business return on your service-oriented architecture (SOA) investment? Are you a business manager who has been disappointed by an information technology (IT) project, or an IT manager or architect who has been disappointed by the business's reaction to your project? If your answer is yes to any of these questions, I wrote this book for you.

If you've been part of one of these disappointing projects, most likely the reason for your disappointment was a disconnect between the business and IT communities—a disconnect that resulted in the project failing to deliver the business value that both sides expected. It is likely that this disconnect was not even recognized until late in the project. So late that a lot of concrete had been poured over the misunderstandings and misconceptions. So late that correcting these misunderstandings and misconceptions began to look like another project.

Such disconnects are simply intolerable in service-oriented architectures. Obtaining a solid return on a SOA investment requires more than simply avoiding such disconnects. It demands proactive and constructive communications between the business and IT communities. The business must clearly define the business objectives of the SOA initiative—the things that will provide the actual business return on the SOA investment.

The business and IT communities must then join forces and work together to achieve these objectives. Together, they must define the business process and system changes required to produce the expected business results. This collaboration is not just to make SOA initiatives succeed. It is essential for any project that is supposed to produce business value. For the most part, failed projects are projects that have either lost sight of the business objectives or failed to focus the business process and system changes on achieving those objectives.

The challenge here is that business processes and information systems have become so intertwined that it is literally impossible to make changes to one without altering the other. In particular, changes to information systems alter business processes—often in unexpected and undesirable ways. Despite this, project plans rarely stop to actually consider the design of business processes, unless the project happens to be tackling a major business process reengineering effort. As a result, business processes just sort of evolve, piecemeal, project by project, as you make changes to your information systems.

When the scope of a project lies entirely within a single business unit, you can get away with this. Working within that business unit, the business users and developers sit down and discuss how it's going to work, and the developers go off and update the systems. This casual approach works reasonably well when there is only one development group and only one user group. However, this approach is woefully inadequate when there are multiple user groups, multiple development groups, and multiple systems involved. In fact, it is a recipe for disaster.

Service-oriented architectures are supposed to bring an end to this chaos. SOA is supposed to provide clean, well-defined interfaces between business entities—between service providers and service consumers. But who, exactly, are those service providers and service consumers? Are they systems? Well, yes and no. There are, indeed, systems providing and consuming services. However, those systems are providing functionality on behalf of business units for use by other business units. Thus, when you define business services, you are actually defining the boundaries between business units and the interfaces between them. In other words, you are defining the structure and organization—the very architecture—of your business units.

The architecture of business units is not a technical issue—it is a business issue. *SOA determines the architecture of both business units and systems!* Consequently, both business and IT need to work together to successfully implement SOA.

A Closer Look

Taking another look at those failed projects, a couple of questions arise. Which projects failed? Most likely the ones that involved multiple business units. Why did they fail? They failed because nobody on the business side of the house thought out what the business process needed to be and how the various business units and systems ought to participate in that process. Or, if they did, they failed to succinctly communicate this understanding to the IT developers.

Either way, this left the IT developers—often multiple groups of developers—guessing as they defined the dialogs between information systems belonging to different business units. Guessing about what the overall business process was supposed to be and guessing about how it should handle exceptions. They implemented these guesses, and only then were the inadequacies of the guesswork recognized. Then they began the arduous process of evolving these business processes into something that actually worked on a business level—as the project slipped into cost overruns and delays.

Let me ask you a question. Would you consider automating the interactions between your enterprise and one of its suppliers without first coming to an agreement about what those interactions would be? How the quote-order-shipment-payment process would actually work? Of course not. Then why on earth should you treat the internal dialog between your business units—your order management group, your warehouse management group, and your financial group—any differently?

Let's be clear about this. I'm not talking about massive business process reengineering. I'm simply talking about taking the time to think out the business process, thinking through what the business process ought to look like and how the business units and information systems will participate in that process. You need this picture to include both sunny-day scenarios and exception handling, and then convince yourself that this vision will produce the business value you expect from the project. Then, and only then, should you make an investment in implementing the business process and system changes.

Why is this important? Because it is business processes that actually provide value to the enterprise. Yes, information systems are an increasingly important component of those business processes, but there is no inherent business value in the systems themselves. Their value lies entirely in their ability to make business processes work. Business processes are what is important. The reason we do IT projects is to make business processes provide more value.

Oops! I slipped (on purpose). In that last paragraph, I made the very mistake I am trying to help you avoid! I said that business processes are important—and then immediately started talking about IT projects.

This thinking, that there is a separation or schism between business and IT, has become an institutionalized habit in many enterprises. It usually extends all the way up to the very top of the organizational hierarchy. Yet this same business–IT separation or schism is the root cause of many project failures.

This schism is an outright showstopper for SOA. This is why architects, business managers, and IT managers, from the frontlines to the chief operating officer (COO) and chief information officer (CIO), need to work together to solve this problem. You are the only ones who can provide the solution.

So what am I asking you to do? If you are a manager, you can help by doing these four things.

1. *Understand the nature of the problem*. Business process architecture determines how business units interact with one another to make business processes work. Systems architecture determines how systems interact with one another to make the technical part of the business process work. Business processes and systems have become so intertwined that you can't design one without designing the other. Thus, business process architecture and systems architecture are but two different views of the same architecture—the total architecture.

2. *Put someone in charge of your total architecture*. If you are to make sense of and manage your enterprise's total architecture, somebody needs to own it—all of it. Business process architecture and systems architecture belong together, under one roof. Today systems architecture is in the IT organization, and as for business process architecture—well, nobody owns that! Don't believe me? Try to find someone in your organization who can describe your complete order-to-cash business process! Then ask yourself how you are supposed to manage something you can't even describe. You need to put someone in charge of your total architecture and get it under control.

3. *Demand total architecture visibility*. Demand that the architecture of your business processes and systems be captured in a form that can be readily understood and shared. Only then will it be possible to have meaningful discussions about modifying and improving business processes before you incur the cost of actually implementing the changes.

4. *Provide the authority needed to manage the total architecture.* To be effective, the group managing the total architecture needs to report to the business operations manager responsible for executing business processes. This is the only person who (a) sets the enterprise priorities and (b) has the authority to command cooperation and change in both the business and IT sides of the house. You don't need to do a massive reorganization. But you do need to take leadership personnel from business and IT, task them with rationalizing and managing how your business actually works, and support them with the authority to make it work.

If you are a business process or systems architect, take action in these ways.

1. *Understand the depths of the interdependencies between business processes and systems.* From determining the functional boundaries between business units and systems to determining the performance requirements and appropriate level of investment in fault tolerance and high availability, all system requirements are derived from an understanding of the business process. These are your responsibilities.

2. *Understand the ultimate dependency of systems upon people for flexibility.* Understand the importance of feedback in detecting and responding to breakdowns in business processes and systems.

3. *Understand the social and organizational issues surrounding your work.* Understand the extent to which your work depends on the cooperation of all organizations involved. Be on the lookout for signs of misaligned priorities, and take action to raise the visibility of these misalignments.

4. *Understand how to efficiently organize a total architecture development.* Understand the importance of providing early feedback regarding cost and schedule feasibility.

5. *Execute every project from the total architecture perspective to provide true business value.* Design business processes and systems together to deliver expected business benefits.

Succeeding with SOA is a call to action for both managers and architects.

For managers, the call is to set the organizational stage to actively manage your total architecture. Architecting your business is a business activity, not an IT activity. The business side of the house needs to take ownership and lead this effort. Put someone in charge of designing and documenting your overall business processes! They are, after all, the lifeblood of your enterprise. Don't leave them to chance.

For architects, the call is to realize that you are architecting business units and business processes as well as systems, and to structure your work accordingly. This volume will help you understand the context for your work. The companion volume, *SOA in Practice: Implementing Total Architecture*, will give you the tools and techniques for actually developing a total architecture.

About the Cover

An ironic coincidence arose during the production of this book in the form of an unintended linkage between the cover art and the book's dedication. The cover art uses strings to show complex linkages between people. To me, this image is an appropriate visual analogy for the complex relationships between individuals and organizations that we find in our everyday business processes. Understanding these relationships and using that understanding to guide the design of both business processes and systems is the focal point of this book. The visual analogy could not be better.

Now, the irony. William Cady Stone, to whom the book is dedicated, was a Professor of Mathematics at Union College. One of his hobbies was using string models to visually illustrate complex mathematical relationships. In addition to the models he constructed himself, he painstakingly restored Union College's collection of the original Olivier Models dating from the nineteenth century. You can visit Union's web site at www.union.edu/Academics/Special/Olivier/ to learn more about Professor Stone and the Olivier models.

Acknowledgments

I would like to thank the many individuals who helped to make this work and this book possible. I give thanks to my mentors who helped me learn how to explore uncharted territory: John Reschovsky, Joel Sturman, David Oliver, David Musser, and Mukkai Krishnamoorthy. I thank my colleagues who have provided an intellectual foil for these ideas: Jonathan Levant, John Hutchison, James Rumbaugh, Michael Blaha, and William Premerlani. For their support of my enterprise

William Cady Stone. (Photograph by John Ross, Schenectady, NY. Reprinted with permission of the Stone family.)

methodology work, I thank Brian Pierce, Bruce Johnson, and Paul Beduhn. For their help in sharpening the real-world architectural concepts, I thank Paul Asmar, David Leigh, Saul Caganoff, and Janet Strong. For helping me turn a concept into a book, I thank Michael Blaha and William Premerlani. For helping me turn the book into a reality, I thank Paul Asmar, Ram Menon, Roger Strukhoff, Scott Fingerhut, Peter Gordon, and Donna Davis. Last, but far from least, I would like to thank my wife, Maria, for her patience, love, and support while bringing this book to life.

PCB
Schenectady, NY
January 2007

Part I

Building Your SOA

Chapter 1

The SOA Challenge

Business processes and information systems have become so tightly intertwined that it is no longer possible to design one without designing the other. Business processes do not simply depend on information systems—they define the services required.

Altering business processes inevitably requires system changes. Conversely, system changes inexorably alter business processes. Herein we find the SOA challenge—designing systems in such a way that accommodating most business process changes simply requires rearranging existing business services. If you can accomplish this, you will not only reduce development costs but will also decrease the time-to-market for these business process changes and thereby improve your enterprise's competitive position.

But business processes involve more than just the functionality of systems. They involve information. Information is central to business processes, and these processes determine what information is required and how it should be managed. Requisitions, orders, claims, and reports, for example, are nothing more than information.

Business processes also depend on people, particularly for decision making and exception handling. From simple work tasks and approvals all the way up to strategic decision making, people provide the flexibility that enables business processes to deal with unexpected emerging opportunities and unanticipated problems. From soothing a disgruntled customer to coping with mergers and acquisitions, people make the difference.

Business processes, people, information, and systems together comprise the symbiotic collaboration that makes the enterprise work. Independently, they accomplish nothing. Together, they bring the enterprise to life. It is this partnership that enables the enterprise to produce its results and achieve its goals.

When you build a service-oriented architecture, you package a significant portion of the systems functionality and related information in the form of services. A *service* is a bundling of information and the functionality required to manage it. An order management service, for example, provides operations for placing, revising, and canceling orders as well as for checking order status. The service manages the order information, including ensuring the durability of the information.

Packaging information in the form of services presents a serious challenge because enterprise goals are not static. They are in constant flux. Changing business pressures and emerging opportunities continually force enterprises to reevaluate and reprioritize goals. When these goals change, enterprises must then refocus this collaboration of business processes, people, information, and systems on the new priorities. This reprioritization needs to be efficient. The ability to respond to new opportunities and changing pressures is, itself, a critical success factor for the enterprise. To quote Thomas Paine (in a phrase later made famous by Lee Iacocca), we can "Lead, follow, or get out of the way." We want to lead. This book will show you how.

The Concept of Total Architecture

Here's the challenge: Organize the collaboration between business processes, people, information, and systems, and focus it on achieving enterprise goals. Design the services in such a way that they facilitate rather than hinder the reorganization and refocusing of the enterprise business processes. Oh, and by the way, do it quickly and efficiently.

To make your enterprises work effectively, business processes, people, information, and systems must be architected together, as a whole. This is *total architecture*. This approach is not a choice. It is a concession to reality. Attempts to organize business processes, people, information, and systems independently result in services that do not fit together particularly well. The modification of business processes becomes inefficient, and the focus on the real business objective gets lost.

When business processes cannot efficiently evolve, enterprises find themselves hamstrung as they try to respond to changing opportunities and pressures. They produce inefficient, fragile, error-prone business processes that seem to defy attempts to improve them. As enterprises grow in scope and complexity, architects embed information systems even more deeply into the business processes to help manage this complexity. The web of people, processes, information, and systems becomes increasingly tangled. So, you have no choice but to address the *total* architecture. The only question is how best to do it.

Total architecture defines the structure and organization of business processes as well as information systems. This is a business responsibility, not an IT responsibility. Because of the interdependency between business processes and systems, this work must be done in concert with the systems architecture. Architecture is no longer just an IT issue—it is an enterprise issue.

Systems Are More Than Services

Systems functionality goes beyond simply providing services. When a business process employs services, some participant in that business process needs to decide when and how each service is employed. We commonly refer to this logic as *service orchestration*. This service orchestration itself is not, necessarily, a service, although many services (known as composite services) will employ service orchestration.

The vast majority of the functionality in your enterprise systems today is not provided in the form of services, and it is unrealistic to think that you can turn all of this functionality into services magically overnight. You must be able to employ this legacy functionality in your business processes just as effectively and efficiently as with your well-designed services. Where appropriate, you also want to evolve this legacy functionality into services.

So while services are the major focus here, there must also be a notion of architecture that is inclusive of service orchestration and nonservice functionality.

Services Involve More Than Business Functionality

When you think of a service, your thoughts probably trend toward the business functionality provided by the service. After all, an order entry service is all about placing and managing orders. But closely related to this business functionality are a bunch of rules regarding the use of the service. Who is authorized to place orders? Who can examine order status? Who is authorized to approve orders?

The rules surrounding the use of services themselves involve additional information and functionality. This information and functionality are also part of the service, and these elements are subject to change as business processes change. In fact, if you look at business process evolution, these rules seem to change more often than the functionality whose use they govern!

While you want business rules to govern access to services, you also want to minimize the technical constraints for accessing them. For the greatest flexibility, you want universal access to your services, rather than having decisions regarding implementation technology or deployment location inadvertently constrain the use of the service. So, for example, you want services implemented in COBOL on mainframes to be as accessible from business process management (BPM) tools and Java-based application servers as they are from within the mainframe itself.

You need location independence in addition to technology independence. For example, a global bank needs to be able to provide services for its customers no matter where they happen to be, for example. A customer from North America should be able to walk into a bank in Europe or Asia and use the banking services as readily as if he or she were at home. From the systems perspective, this means that the local banking system needs to be able to access customer information regardless of the actual location of the service that happens to have information for that specific customer.

This need to alter access rules flexibly and provide ubiquitous access to services in turn drives the architecture of individual services toward a modular design. This modularity separates business functionality from access rules and routing rules, while providing uniform service access from any technology. These are the core service architecture requirements that will enable you to independently alter business functionality, access policies, and routing rules.

Growing Pressures

Business processes have long spanned the multiple silos found within enterprises (Figure 1–1). Then why are you starting to experience more

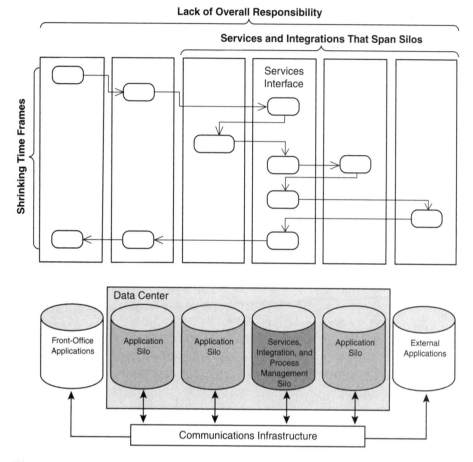

Figure 1–1: *Sources of Pressure*

significant problems now? The answer is that changes afoot within enterprises are stressing their existing architectures.

The majority of IT projects have traditionally focused on a single business process activity (or group of activities) residing entirely within a single application silo. The project's focus is generally to improve this activity's functionality, cut its cost, or improve its response time. The entire project generally lives within the silo: business objective, justification, budget, and staff.

Evolving business pressures have begun to force you to take a different view. One of these pressures is to improve the responsiveness of the enterprise as a whole. Customers and business partners want the business to respond more quickly. They want to have ordered goods delivered tomorrow (or today), not next week. They want the status of their order when they ask, not a callback in an hour after someone has investigated. The problem, of course, is that such projects require changes in multiple silos. They do not fit well within existing project structures.

Another major pressure is cost management. The wide adaptation to enterprise resource planning (ERP), for example, has sought to optimize resource utilization by coordinating and managing all enterprise-wide business processes related to planning, procurement, and production. These efforts impact all of the architectural elements, and successful ERP projects address them all, in concert. Projects that treat ERP solely as an IT initiative inexorably, and spectacularly, fail.

There are also increasing pressures to increase the return on investment (ROI) from IT projects and to make systems and business processes more flexible. This has pushed SOA to the forefront as enterprises seek to architect business processes from reusable services. The vision is that the reuse of services will cut IT costs by avoiding the cost of reimplementing existing functionality in future projects. Services also promise the potential for implementing new (or revised) business processes more quickly by simply composing existing services. This not only reduces IT costs but cuts the overall time span of the project as well. It improves an enterprise's ability to respond to outside pressures.

The sticking point here is that business services are pieces of business processes. They involve people and information as well as systems. In defining business services, you are structuring and organizing (i.e., architecting) business processes and business organizations as well as systems. If services are to be reused, they must fit cleanly into multiple business processes and align well with assigned business responsibilities. They require the total architecture perspective and active business involvement.

Business services also pose challenges to existing silo-based project structures. A business service encapsulates functionality provided by one business unit so that it can be used by at least one other business unit. That other business unit is responsible for some other portion of the overall business process. In order for this to work, the interests and needs of these other business units must be factored into the design of the business service, or it will not provide the functionality required.

This multiple-business-unit perspective does not fit well into traditional silo-oriented IT projects. To begin with, the service provider does not accrue any of the benefits of reuse. In fact, the silo implementing the business service will actually incur a higher initial cost for providing its functionality as a service. Nor does the first user accrue any benefit unless the reuse actually occurs within this first project. It is generally the second and subsequent projects that will realize the benefits of services. Existing project structures are not designed to handle projects that span multiple silos and whose benefits will be realized only in the future.

Framing the Challenges

It is clear that responding to these pressures requires projects that span multiple business units. This requirement challenges almost every aspect of the way enterprises conduct projects today. In contrast to traditional projects, these new projects require coordinating the work of multiple business units in order to achieve enterprise goals. This coordination is required both in defining the business processes and in the systems development work needed to get those business processes ready for execution. These projects are doing nothing less than modifying the total architecture of the business.

At the heart of this modification lies the determination of who should be doing what in the revised business process: what work should be done by people, and what work should be done by systems. Since both people and systems live in organizational silos, this determination decides what each silo will be responsible for in the revised process. This, in turn, will determine what development work each silo needs to do in order to implement the revised business process.

Therein lies the problem with current project structures. Who, in silo-oriented projects, has the responsibility for revising the total architecture—both business processes and systems? Who defines the needed services? Who has the responsibility for determining the operational and developmental responsibilities for each silo? Who has the authority to make the silos cooperate in this endeavor? How is the overall budget determined and allocated to the silos?

In most enterprises, the silo-based development processes do not contain explicit tasks for determining who should be doing what—either during development or in the revised business process. They have development processes similar to the one shown in Figure 1–2. You either give the requirements to the silo's development team or tell the team to go determine what the requirements are. If there is any figuring out to be done, the silo's development team does this work. If there is work required in other silos, the development team negotiates with the other silos to get that work done. The silo owns the entire project.

The problem you will encounter with SOA projects is that this streamlined client-server development process doesn't scale. You can't just hand a set of requirements to several development teams, ask each team to figure out what services it ought to be creating, and expect to have an efficient development process that also meets business goals. In fact, with such a fragmented approach, no one is actually accountable for achieving the overall business goals. How can we expect to achieve business goals without such a focus?

An alternative development process looks something like the one shown in Figure 1–3. The project begins with an explicit process charter that provides the vision and focus for the overall effort. This charter sets forth the project goals; establishes the project's cost, schedule, and other constraints; and assigns the key project leadership responsibilities. This process contains an explicit step for determining the services required—the architecture activity. It contains a concession to reality as well: an explicit integration test step. It is impractical to simply turn on a large-scale system with many services for the first time and begin testing. For efficiency, the system needs to be integrated in an organized manner, a few services at a time.

The idea of having a clearly defined project charter, an explicit architecture step, and an integration test step is not new by any means. Their inclusion in the development process is a well-established best practice for software development. But if these steps are no longer present in your development process, you must reintroduce them. In addition, your thinking about the scope of the project and its related

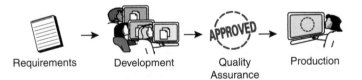

Requirements   Development   Quality   Production
                                           Assurance

Figure 1–2: *Silo-Based Client-Server Development*

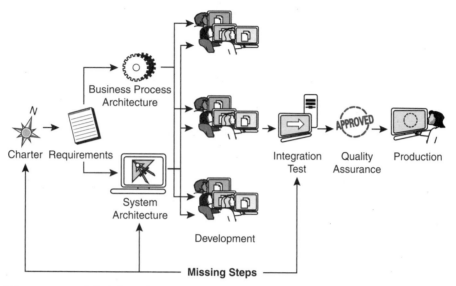

Figure 1–3: *SOA Development*

architecture activity must be extended to encompass business process design as well as system design.

The architecture step is the key to making SOA development work. In this activity, the business process architect determines what services and service orchestrations are needed in the revised business process in order to achieve the business goals. At the same time, the systems architect determines how these services and orchestrations will be provided—and what legacy functionality is required. Together, the architectural responsibilities span both business processes and information systems, both development time and runtime. This step encompasses all of the elements of total architecture.

Closely related to this development process challenge is an organizational challenge (Figure 1–4): Who has overall ownership of a project that spans multiple business units? Who is responsible for the architecture step that determines what each silo should be doing? Where, organizationally, do they report?

This project ownership problem is exacerbated further by a commonplace organizational approach used when introducing new technologies into the enterprise: creating a new IT silo just for the new technology! Unfortunately, this silo, unlike the application silos, does not have a business counterpart (as indicated by the question mark in

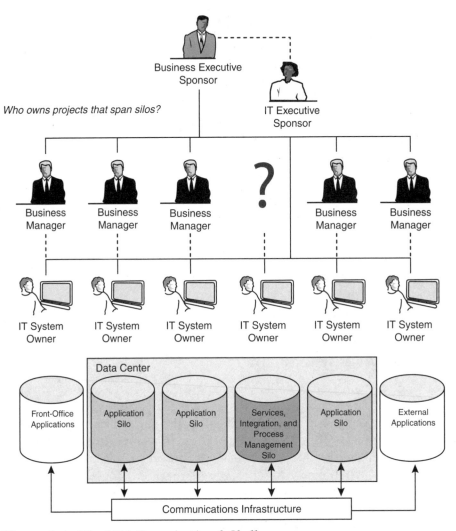

Figure 1–4: *The SOA Organizational Challenge*

Figure 1–4). Yet you expect this silo to use the new technology to integrate the other silos. You make it responsible for services, service orchestration, integration, and process management. Yet unless you give it a business side, with authority over the silos involved, you have not created a recipe for success.

Some enterprises are aware of the project ownership issue and the need for overall business guidance in silo-spanning projects. This is evidenced in the structuring of major initiatives like ERP. The business creates a program office that reports to senior management and is responsible for the overall initiative. Successful ERP programs not only address the total architecture issues but also have the authority to ensure the cooperative participation of all the silos involved.

The problem is that more and more projects span multiple silos. In fact, service-oriented architectures make such projects the norm, not the exception. So you need an organizational home for projects that span multiple silos. This home must acknowledge that these silo-spanning projects are deep collaborations between business and IT. SOA projects are not IT projects—they are business projects that have a major IT component.

The final challenge is posed by the notion of reusable services. While you may develop a service in one project, the intent should be to design that service so that it can be reused in subsequent projects (Figure 1–5). Who can provide this cross-project perspective? Who can determine where else the service might be used? Who can look ahead to future projects and anticipate their needs accurately enough to specify a service that will actually satisfy those needs? Who can ensure that future projects will actually use the available services and not reinvent them?

These diverse challenges are all facets of the enterprise's total architecture. Total architecture spans silos. It spans business and IT. It spans projects, both present and future. In fact, total architecture is the core of the enterprise. It is the structure of organizations, business processes, and systems. It is there, whether you like it or not. So you have a choice. You can choose to turn your back and plod on in ignorance—or you can recognize total architecture for what it is: the very structure of your enterprise. That's what this book is all about.

Staying on Track

There are four keys to staying on track with the total architecture approach to SOA. The first is to *justify each project on its own business merits*. Each project should make business sense on its own. It should tackle specific business problems with measurable objectives and constraints. It should identify the business processes that need to be modified in order to achieve its objectives. It should maintain focus on modifying those business processes to achieve the business objectives,

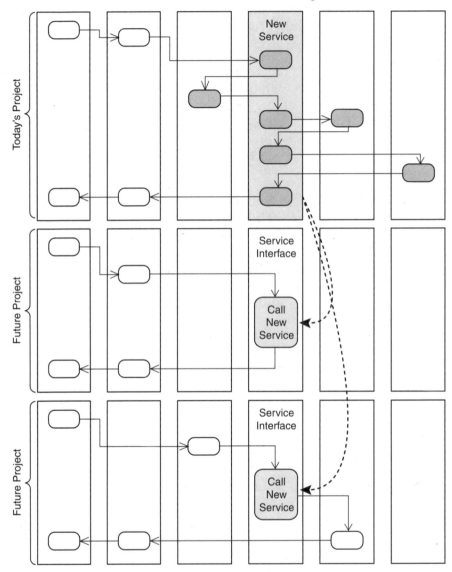

Figure 1–5: *Cross-Project SOA Challenges*

doing so within the project's cost and schedule constraints. Organizing projects around business objectives and business processes ensures that each project yields a recognizable business value and justifies its own cost.

The second key is to *have an explicit architecture step* in every SOA project that precedes the actual development work. In this step, you consider ways in which the business process participants might collaborate to get the job done and select the approach you will actually take. Some of these participants will be providing services, while others orchestrate the use of services and access legacy systems. It's a shell game, with the participants (both people and systems) being the shells and their responsibility assignments being the peas. Once you select a satisfactory architecture, you will have a detailed inventory of the required development work. From this, you can determine the cost and then know whether the project can produce the expected business benefit within the given cost and schedule guidelines. This sequence is total architecture at work.

The third key is to *have an active SOA architecture group*. Total architecture spans all projects and all silos. The results of each project must integrate smoothly with those of others. In fact, this is the prime requirement for service-oriented architectures—services must fit smoothly into future projects. In order to achieve this, someone must have the responsibility to determine how these pieces will fit together and to shape them accordingly, with the authority to ensure project compliance. This is the role of the SOA architecture group.

The SOA architecture group is responsible for the total architecture of the enterprise. It establishes the vision of where the enterprise is going in terms of both business process architecture and systems architecture. It is responsible, directly or indirectly, for the common infrastructure, shared services, best practices, and architectural patterns employed in the enterprise. The SOA architecture group is not an ivory-tower organization. It gets its hands dirty making sure that the work of each project integrates smoothly into the enterprise architecture. It does this through a combination of direct participation, training, mentoring, and governance reviews.

The fourth key is to *have a living SOA project roadmap*. The roadmap lays out the plan for present and future projects, with a two- to three-year planning horizon. It not only lays out a sequence of projects based on business priorities but also lays out the roadmap for services development: which projects will produce which services, and which future projects are expected to employ those services. This roadmap is a joint effort between the business leadership team, the IT leadership team, and the SOA architecture group.

These four keys provide the strategy for succeeding with SOA. The roadmap plans the services development. The SOA architecture group ensures that services are well conceived. The architecture step ensures that they are used appropriately. Most importantly, justifying each project on its own business merit makes it possible to sustain the investment in services indefinitely. This·winning formula has been time-tested in top global and Fortune 500 companies.

How to Use This Book

This book is the first of a pair of closely related books on SOA and total architecture. This book is targeted at the enterprise leadership community. Its purpose is to illustrate why total architecture is critical to enterprise success and the roles that the leadership team must play to make SOA work. The second book is aimed at SOA architects. Its purpose is to arm project and enterprise architects with the knowledge and tools they need to build and manage the enterprise's total architecture.

This book, *Succeeding with SOA*, presents service-oriented architecture from the management perspective. It illustrates what can happen to enterprise business processes and projects when elements of the total architecture are neglected. It explores the deepening reliance of business processes on information systems and the resulting need to keep SOA projects focused on achieving well-defined business objectives within cost and schedule guidelines. It examines the challenges posed by organizational structures and shows how paying attention to five key leadership roles can bring the SOA focus to the enterprise without requiring significant reorganization.

This book also shows how a SOA architecture group can provide continuity and consistency across projects while maintaining an overall focus on enterprise objectives such as reaping the benefits of service-oriented architectures. It explores how the robustness of business processes can be improved by paying attention to the simple structure of the interservice dialog within the process. It illustrates how an understanding of business risk can be used to guide investments in fault tolerance and high availability. It outlines an agile approach to SOA that can efficiently produce a robust architecture, with accurate early determination as to whether the business objectives can be achieved within the cost and schedule guidelines. Finally, it looks at successfully structuring, initiating, and executing SOA projects with the total architecture perspective.

Succeeding with SOA will be followed shortly by a second book, *SOA in Practice: Implementing Total Architecture*. This companion volume is the how-to book for SOA architects. Although the book is organized as a progression of issues that the project architect must address, each chapter also discusses the related activities of the enterprise SOA architecture group. It explores the modeling of business processes and the information they depend on and discusses nonfunctional requirements in the context of the business processes to which they pertain. It covers service-oriented architecture, starting with the high-level structuring problem, and then adds successive levels of detail pertaining to communications, data, coordination, breakdown detection, high availability, fault tolerance, load distribution, security, and monitoring.

The companion volume discusses architecture evaluation, detailing the architecture with specifications, and the role the architect must play in testing. It then delves into some of the more complex aspects of a service-oriented architecture: complex business processes, business process monitoring, business process management and workflow, and large-scale business services. It concludes with a summary discussion of the SOA architecture group, the role it plays, and the challenges it faces.

You can use these books in two very different ways. One way is prescriptive. Together, the two volumes present a structured approach that you can use to organize and conduct both individual projects and an overall service-oriented architecture effort. The other way is as an assessment and review guideline. Each chapter addresses a specific topic and concludes with a list of key questions related to that topic. You can use these questions as a self-evaluation guide for your current projects and SOA efforts. Then you can use the body of the chapter to understand more about the specific issues and the various ways in which they can be addressed. Either approach will improve your enterprise's total architecture.

Chapter 2

Business Process Pitfalls

Virtually everything that happens in an enterprise is the result of executing a business process. Filling orders, manufacturing goods, selling mortgages, and providing services all depend on the proper execution of business processes. As these core business processes constitute the very heart of the business, problems with them hurt the enterprise competitively and keep it from achieving its goals.

Despite the wide variety of business processes, there is a surprising similarity in the causes of their failure. What is common to most breakdowns is a simple lack of understanding about what the business process is supposed to be doing and what it is actually doing. In this age of enterprise-scale business processes assembled from loosely coupled services, failures can be insidiously difficult to pinpoint.

Three actions are required to help you understand whether your business processes are working properly: defining the business process, measuring its execution, and comparing the measurements against the process definition. Sound simple? It can be—provided that the end-to-end business process and the services that support it are, in fact, consciously designed with these three objectives in mind. Done right, this understanding also sets the stage for gracefully handling business process breakdowns.

Process Breakdowns Go Undetected

If you don't monitor the business process execution and compare it against the expected process, breakdowns can go undetected until the consequences become too serious to be ignored. Angry customers call to complain about late shipments or poor service, for example. You can address such incidents, but you might never completely recover. Despite your best efforts, customer confidence has been damaged. Meanwhile, productivity is negatively impacted and profitability is down, and all because the process was not being monitored. Let's take a look at a real example.[1]

Case Study

Case Study: Internal Processing of Purchase Requests

The Setting: A high-tech manufacturing company implemented a largely automated internal business process for purchasing raw materials. The goal of the project was to improve profitability by minimizing raw material inventory. To accomplish this, the company implemented a purchasing process that achieves just-in-time delivery of the materials from suppliers. Materials arrive as they are required, eliminating the need for most material inventory and its associated carrying cost.

In this new business process, the production planning system frequently analyzes product demand forecasts and production schedules to determine the need for raw materials. The production planning system then automatically generates purchase requests for the required raw materials. These purchase requests are automatically routed to the purchasing system's workflow, which manages their conversion into purchase orders. Finally, the purchase orders are electronically delivered to vendors and acknowledgments received. (After this, the materials are actually delivered, but this story is about a breakdown in the request-to-order process.)

Because of significant differences in the ways that the production planning system and the purchasing system represent material requests, some fairly complex transformation and mapping operations are required as these requests move between the systems. Furthermore, the volume of these purchase requests requires the distribution of this

---

1. Each case study in this book has been drawn from an actual experience with a top global or Fortune 500 company.

transformation and mapping activity across several content transformation engines. The stage is now set for a business process breakdown.

The Problem: After the new process had been running for a number of months, someone noticed that occasionally the output of the content transformation process was not what it ought to be. In order to enable detailed tracing of the business logic, a modified copy of the transformation process was brought up in a test environment. Unfortunately, although this modified copy was in the test environment, it was brought up *with the actual production configuration.* As a result, it happily accepted its fair share of material requests from the production planning system. However, *due to the debugging modifications, it did not deliver them to the purchasing system!* Real production material requests were being lost. This was the breakdown in the process—but it was not immediately detected.

Four days later, the production facility noticed that some of the needed raw materials were not being delivered when required. The production line had to be shut down. An initial investigation quickly revealed that some of the material requests that had been sent by the production planning system were never received by the purchasing system.

Unfortunately, this initial investigation did not reveal why or how the purchase requests were lost. After a three-day investigation, someone finally uncovered the fact that this test copy was accepting purchase requests from the production system and essentially throwing them away. Problem solved, but only after a production shutdown.

Lessons Learned: Without the active monitoring of critical business processes, breakdowns can go undetected long enough to cause serious problems for the enterprise.

Production environments should be isolated from test environments to prevent inadvertent interaction between the production environment and other environments.

Service-Level Agreements Are Not Met

The next case study involves service-level agreements (SLAs). Whether agreements are formalized or not, customers and business partners always have expectations about how long a given business process will take and the times during which that process will be available. They expect the store to be open during advertised hours and the web site to be up when they visit it. They expect that purchasing an item will not take all day. Customers expect that the books they order will be delivered when promised and that the packages they send via overnight delivery service will actually arrive the next day. They expect that bank deposits will be posted to their accounts at the time the bank says that it will. All of these expectations reflect the reality that, for many customers and business partners, *when* something happens is just as important as *what* happens.

SLAs formalize expectations about the responsiveness and availability of a service. They contractually commit the enterprise to provide services that meet specific responsiveness and availability goals. Typical service-level specifications include the maximum time interval between a request and a response, the availability of a service (the percentage of time the service is available for use), and the maximum allowed outage (the length of time that a service may be unavailable). SLA contracts usually include financial rewards for meeting the specified service levels and/or financial penalties for failing to meet the service levels. Thus, from the service provider's perspective, an SLA represents mandatory performance standards for the enterprise's business processes.

However, simply establishing performance standards does not ensure that the enterprise's business processes will meet those standards. Making certain that SLA commitments are indeed met requires actively monitoring the processes. This monitoring provides the data needed to measure each process's performance and adjust it to achieve the desired performance levels. It also provides a means of detecting breakdowns and responding to them in a timely manner—ideally, before the SLA is violated.

Recovering from a breakdown often requires a number of coordinated actions. In other words, the recovery itself is a process. When service-level agreements specify the maximum outage time for a service, this establishes a time frame within which the company must complete the recovery process.

You ensure that the recovery process executes on time by establishing a deadline for each of the actions in the recovery process, then monitoring their actual execution. You compare the actual completion times against the corresponding deadlines. When there are exceptions (late activities), you can proactively manage the process, accelerating subsequent activities to get the recovery process back on track and ensuring that the overall outage SLA is met.

Managing a service-level agreement for a recovery process gets particularly tricky when the process involves diagnostic activities that are then used to determine the needed recovery actions. The required activities in the latter stages of the recovery process won't even be known until the diagnostic activities have been completed.

Organizational structure can further complicate the execution of a process. In large enterprises, different organizations often perform different activities. Successfully executing such an organizationally fragmented process requires good communication between the organizations, both to monitor the progress of the process and to manage the recovery from process breakdowns. In order for communication to be effective, the needed dialog must be determined in advance and agreed to by all parties. Most importantly, a single organization must own the responsibility for monitoring and managing the overall process.

When activities are outsourced to another company, each activity will typically have an SLA of its own as part of the contract. These activities will require the same level of monitoring and management since they are part of an in-house process. Consequently, the communications for initiating the activities, obtaining timely status feedback, and handling exceptions need to be established and agreed to as part of the outsourcing contract.

Whether activities are performed by your organization, another organization within your enterprise, or an external company, satisfying SLAs requires monitoring and management mechanisms for all activities. When multiple organizations are involved, all interorganizational communications, including those needed for tracking progress and escalating exception handling, must be provided for in advance. Failing to make such provisions can make it nearly impossible to satisfy the SLAs for the overall process.

Case Study

Case Study: Telecommunications Service SLAs

The Setting: This case study involves a company that provides telecommunications services to other companies, including installing private branch exchanges (PBX), designing and installing computer networks, and providing voice and data communications capabilities between sites. The design and operation of these telecommunications services involve complex processes. Each service requires a design effort to determine the equipment and wiring required at various locations, as well as the required configuration of that equipment. Some service changes require the installation of new equipment and wiring, while others require only configuration changes to existing equipment.

The process of providing these services is greatly complicated by the number of organizations involved. The wiring of customer premises is typically contracted out to local companies. Some of the major communications links between sites are themselves services provided by other companies. Even within the telecommunications company itself there are many specialized organizations that handle the installation of customer premises equipment, the installation of local switching centers, the operation of the local switching centers, and the installation of the major trunk lines and related equipment. Each of these organizations, both internal and external, has its own business processes and systems for handling orders and managing its own activities.

Providing services that satisfy stringent SLAs is a major selling point for the company. The entire network of systems and business processes has been specifically designed to satisfy SLA requirements for both service installation and operation. To ensure the achievement of the overall SLA, every activity in the process has an SLA of its own. Even the activities that are part of breakdown recovery processes have their own SLAs to ensure that service to customers is restored within the promised time frame. There should be no problem meeting SLAs—at least on paper.

The Problem: Despite this conscious business process design and its focus on satisfying SLAs, customers frequently complain that their service-level agreements are not being satisfied. Specifically, when a service outage occurs, service is often not restored within the specified SLA time frame. Customers regularly invoke the penalty clauses in their SLAs, and this is costing the company millions of dollars.

In investigating the problems, the company discovered that the tracking of the recovery process activities only records the successful completion of the activities. Completely absent is any reporting or identification of activities that have *not* been completed on time. In the absence of such identification, the company has no mechanism to get delayed recovery processes back on track. The result is that any breakdown in the recovery process generally remains undetected until the customer SLA is violated, at which point the customer complains and the company loses money.

Lessons Learned: When SLAs are involved, simply monitoring the primary business activity to detect breakdowns is often not enough: The process of recovering from breakdowns must also be monitored for proper execution. Breakdown detection and appropriate escalations need to be designed into the recovery process to ensure that it executes in a manner that preserves the agreed-upon SLA.

Process Changes Do Not Produce Expected Benefits

A third case study explores what can happen when you try to make business process improvements without fully understanding the actual business process. How this can come about is quite natural. Business process evolution usually begins with the identification of some portion of the process that is a source of pain for the enterprise. That portion of the process is then analyzed and reengineered to improve it.

But focusing too narrowly on a small portion of a business process may not solve the overall problem. Improving one part of the process may just expose some other portion as a problem area. Thus, making local improvements may not provide a substantial improvement in the overall business process.

A common (and expensive) form of ad hoc business process "improvement" is to expedite the movement of work (e.g., an order) through a business process. You assign a person to expedite a particular request through the process. This person alters selected portions of the process to try to speed things up, selecting those portions requiring attention based on a current understanding of the process. But the business process understanding is often flawed, and such attempts frequently meet with failure.

Case Study

Case Study: Expediting Orders

The Setting: This case study involves a manufacturer of power generation equipment—the type that provides electrical power to cities. Acquiring these machines and putting them into service is a lengthy process. The interval of time between a power company's decision to add generation capacity and the actual placement of the equipment into service can easily span a decade, and the order-to-delivery process for the machine itself can span several years.

The machines are expensive, running into the hundreds of millions of dollars for one capable of generating as much as a gigawatt of power (enough to power nearly a million households). While there are a relatively small number of basic designs of this type of equipment, each machine's design is tailored to achieve optimum fuel efficiency at its intended location, taking climate and altitude into consideration. Small changes in efficiency translate into many millions of dollars per year in fuel costs.

Power generation equipment is designed to have a very long operational life, typically 40 years or more. During the equipment's lifetime, the design continues to evolve both to improve efficiency and to correct problems. This evolution presents a business process challenge when providing spare parts for older machines. In order to incorporate design improvements that have been made since a machine was initially manufactured, each replacement part order for that machine must be reviewed by engineering staff. This review ensures that the latest improvements are incorporated into the design of the replacement part before it is manufactured.

The same engineering personnel that design new machines also handle the engineering of replacement parts. This work is scheduled in with the normal production work. Similarly, the replacement parts are manufactured in the same production facilities as the new machines and scheduled in with the normal production manufacturing.

Recently, the company has come under pressure from competitors that specialize in providing custom-manufactured replacement parts for power generation equipment—and providing them quickly. These competitors are starting to take a significant share of the replacement parts business for certain types of parts.

To address this challenge, the company is in the process of reevaluating and redesigning its engineering and manufacturing planning systems. However, implementing these changes will take some time. None of the systems, from order entry through engineering planning and manufacturing resource planning, have been designed to distinguish spare and renewal parts orders and prioritize the handling of replacement parts orders.

While the required changes will take years to implement, the business cannot afford to wait that long before responding to this competitive challenge. To address the challenge in the short term, the company has created a new business role: expediter. These people are responsible for expediting spare and renewal parts orders from critical customers.

The Problem: In this case study, a replacement parts order is received from an important customer. In order to make a favorable impression on the customer, the company decides to expedite the order with an aggressive delivery date.

The expediter follows the order through engineering. After the decision is made to update the part design, the expediter literally stands over the shoulder of the draftsperson as the revised manufacturing drawing for the part is produced. As soon as the drawing is completed, the expediter personally makes a copy of the drawing, hand carries it to the shop foreperson, and directs her to manufacture the part as soon as possible. Mission accomplished—or is it?

The foreperson, in turn, passes the drawing on to the machinist who will make the part. The machinist is directed to begin after he finishes the part he is currently working on—which takes several days because these parts are not simple. Unfortunately, when the machinist is ready to begin the work on the new part, the raw material needed is not on hand!

What happened? Unknowingly, the expediter, by taking the drawing directly to the shop floor, has actually bypassed a portion of the business process. Specifically, he bypassed the part of the process that provides the raw materials. Normally, when a replacement part design is completed, the drafting administrator makes *two* copies of the drawing. One of these copies goes to the shop, but the other copy goes to the materials organization. The materials organization then obtains the necessary materials and delivers them to the shop at the scheduled time.

In the failed expediting of the replacement part, the materials organization was not even informed that materials were required. The subsequent delays in acquiring the material resulted in a missed delivery date. The customer was very annoyed—and rightly so. Unscheduled delays in returning power generation equipment to service can cost millions of dollars per day. As a consequence of this missed promise date, millions of dollars of replacement parts orders were lost to the competitor. This loss occurred because the business process for providing the replacement part was not understood to begin with.

Lessons Learned: Trying to speed up (or otherwise improve) a business process without fully understanding the entire end-to-end process may fail to improve the overall process—and may make it worse. Such changes may simply expose some other portion of the process as a critical path or limiting factor in the process's performance.

Summary

Managing a process—any process—requires an understanding of what that process is (or is supposed to be). This becomes even more critical when you want to employ information systems to manage or automate your business processes. Unfortunately, the actual end-to-end enterprise business processes, particularly those in large siloed organizations, tend to be poorly understood.

It is surprisingly unusual to find anyone who accurately understands an end-to-end business process in its entirety. Often, individuals understand portions of the process in great detail, but the big picture is another matter entirely. This poses a challenge. If you want to improve the overall business processes, someone needs to first understand the process. You need to assign this responsibility and determine where it belongs in your organization. This is absolutely essential when you want information systems to assume responsibility for all or part of the business process. Without this understanding, it is impossible to have confidence that the changes you are making will have the desired effect.

Understanding your business processes is an essential prerequisite to building the information systems needed to bring these business processes to life.

Key Business Process Questions

1. How can you tell that your critical business processes are operating properly?
2. How can you tell that your processes are meeting their SLA commitments and other performance goals?
3. How can you recover from business process breakdowns without disappointing your customers?
4. Who in your enterprise understands the overall business process well enough to be able to predict what will happen when you modify a portion of the process?

Suggested Reading

Harmon, Paul. 2003. *Business Process Change: A Manager's Guide to Improving, Redesigning, and Automating Processes.* San Francisco, CA: Morgan Kaufmann.

Chapter 3

Business Systems Pitfalls

It is an unfortunate but well-documented fact that many IT projects never make it into production. Some seem to grow like cancers, continually growing in scope as they consume time and resources but never producing a usable result. Others make it to user acceptance testing only to get the "That's not what I wanted!" reaction from the user community. Even systems that do make it into production often do not provide the full benefit that was expected. Some provide only marginal benefit. Others may actually provide the expected benefit but have overrun their cost and schedule to the point where their benefits no longer justify the expenditure.

Projects such as these are detrimental to the business. Development work that provides only marginal benefits or never makes it into production is an unwise investment. Such projects not only fail to give the expected return on their investment, they also waste resources that might have been applied toward achieving other goals. Failed projects also cause the business to lose confidence that business improvement goals can actually be established and realized. The credibility of the IT organization (or at least its current management) suffers as well. Most significantly, the business problem that motivated the project remains unaddressed!

A substantial portion of this book is devoted to approaching projects in such a way that these types of failures can never happen. In preparation, it's useful to view a couple of real-world examples of project failures to gain some insight as to how these situations arise.

Where's the Beef? Projects That Don't Deliver Tangible Benefits

A major cause of project abandonment is the failure of the resulting system to provide any real benefit to the enterprise. How can this happen, when the sole purpose of the project is to provide the benefit? It happens when the project team becomes so caught up in the technical aspects of the problem that it loses sight of the real business need.

Such projects generally fail to engage the business process owners to understand the real business goals and project motivation. They don't look at the problem from a business perspective. They fail to understand the business process changes required to solve the problem. In the absence of true business understanding, the systems are built to reflect the IT organization's perception of the problem. Consequently, the resulting system may not produce a business process that actually solves the business problem. Substantial changes may be required to obtain a workable business solution—changes that carry with them cost overruns and delays.

Failed projects are often not recognized until user acceptance testing. Only at this point does the business side of the house become aware of the business process issues. At a minimum, the system will require significant rework. Often the resulting disappointment results in the project being abandoned altogether.

Case Study

Case Study: Unified Customer Interface

The Setting: This case study involves a large enterprise that has many business units, each of which markets a different service to small businesses. The situation is very confusing for the small-business owners—the customers. They are being approached by many different salespeople from the same company (though from different business units). Sometimes they are approached with competing service offerings—from the same company! When customers need assistance with a particular service, they first need to figure out which business unit to call. The company has received many complaints about this situation and is losing business to competitors.

The enterprise decides to respond to this situation by presenting to customers a unified view of the business. The vision calls for a unified web site, a single phone number to call for help, and sales representatives that are knowledgeable about many service offerings. A new organization is formed for the purpose of creating the web site and the single-phone point of contact.

This organization immediately begins to focus on consolidating the many business unit web sites into a unified framework. Since the new concept has not yet been proven, many of the business units remain skeptical. Consequently, the ground rules for the project are that no changes will be made to any of the existing systems belonging to the individual business units. The new web site must work with the business systems as they presently exist.

The new organization focuses on the technically challenging problem of presenting a consolidated web presence to customers. Based on the existing web sites, it creates a web site with a unified catalog of all the business unit service offerings. The web site design allows small-business owners to navigate the catalog and express interest in specific service offerings. The design has provisions for forwarding the sales leads to the individual business units for follow-up action. It also has a few examples of interfaces to business unit back-office systems that can be used to view the status of accounts and request assistance.

The Problem: The business units are somewhat skeptical about this new effort. As a result, there is a lot of passive resistance to the new organization and its efforts. While a couple of business units reluctantly disclose the technical details of some system interfaces, there is no real discussion of the actual business processes and how the new web site and interfaces impact those business processes. There isn't even a discussion about providing feedback via the web site regarding the status of information requests submitted via the web site.

As a result, the new organization creates a web site capable of integrating with business unit systems, but with no actual integration implemented other than simply forwarding sales leads via e-mail. After nearly a year of work, the site goes live, with all of the features that would have required access to business systems disabled. In particular, the customer's consolidated management view for purchased services is disabled. What is actually deployed is simply a consolidated catalog of service offerings and the ability to request more information.

After this site has been in operation for a few months, it comes time to budget for the following year. Since the new organization does not directly generate any revenue, it must be funded by the other business units. From the business unit's perspective, the only benefit that the new organization provides is another source of sales leads, and this just duplicates their existing web site capabilities. The business units do not see any benefits for themselves in the new endeavor, and they resist further investment in the new organization. As a result, the system is decommissioned and the new organization disbanded. A hundred person-years of effort have been wasted.

Lessons Learned: In order to achieve a tangible business benefit, you must first define that benefit and the business changes necessary to bring it about. Without this definition, there can be no meaningful business direction to the technical effort.

Disparate business processes cannot be coherently integrated unless the business process owners are behind the effort and the required modifications to the business processes are identified and committed to. A technical organization cannot achieve business process integration on its own.

Systems Won't Perform in Production

The early stages of many projects focus almost exclusively on satisfying functional requirements. With an eye toward quickly demonstrating results to the business community, such projects rapidly assemble a system with this functional focus. In these initial efforts, little attention is paid to nonfunctional requirements[1] such as performance and work management. The goal is simply to demonstrate how the system will help a business worker in his or her tasks.

In such projects, it is not until the system has been developed sufficiently to demonstrate functional support that the nonfunctional production requirements are considered. Unfortunately, it is often the case

---

1. Broadly speaking, functional requirements define *what the system is supposed to do.* All other requirements are typically considered nonfunctional requirements. Nonfunctional requirements specify things like performance (throughput and response time), availability (the percentage of time the system is available to perform work), and security (who is authorized to use the system).

that a major rearchitecting of the system will be required in order to accommodate these nonfunctional requirements. Much of the development work will have to be substantially modified. The estimated cost and schedule to complete now skyrocket way beyond the initial budgetary expectations. The credibility of the project team and even the veracity of its new estimates are questioned in light of this lack of foresight. At this point, the project may be canceled due to the lack of confidence in the team and its estimates.

Case Study

Case Study: Fraud Investigation

The Setting: This case study involves a financial institution that needs an improved system to support fraud investigation. The existing system was initially developed as a desktop personal computer (PC) application and later ported to a server platform. Much of the information used in investigations is presently contained in paper folders. Work assignments are made by passing these folders from desk to desk, making it difficult to determine who is responsible for a given investigation.

The current approach is cumbersome from a user interface perspective as well. Investigators must interact with both the fraud investigation system itself and a number of the financial systems in order to conduct their investigation and make accounts adjustments. Their screens are cluttered with many windows into many systems, and they are constantly copying data from one window to another. Mistakes made during copy-and-paste actions are a significant source of errors in the business process. Managing the investigation process is also difficult. The system does not provide enough visibility into the status of individual investigations to effectively schedule and track the work.

The financial institution concludes that it is time to build a new system. This system will do away with the paper fraud investigation folders, making them electronic. Having folders in electronic form will make it possible to manage the work assignments with a workflow engine. The system will also provide a single user interface for the fraud investigators. This will avoid the need for investigators to have many windows open to different systems and will eliminate cut-and-paste errors.

The new system will interact with the other financial systems on behalf of the user to both acquire data and perform account updates. This will not only make it easier for the fraud investigators but also enable the system to track the status of these interactions. The use of workflow in the new system will make it significantly easier to track and reassign work, thus improving the management of the fraud investigation process.

The technical complexity of consolidating the user interfaces and having the new system interact with many other systems generated significant skepticism among the business users about the project feasibility. As a result, a decision was made to demonstrate these functional capabilities as quickly as possible. The early project focused exclusively on implementing the full set of functionality needed to support one individual fraud investigator and demonstrating the required underlying interactions with other systems. An initial version of the system was built to show these capabilities. This development took significantly longer than expected, but the system eventually progressed into user acceptance testing.

The Problem: While the system was, indeed, capable of performing all of the functions required for investigating fraud and managing the process, testing revealed some serious problems. The system performed poorly with significant numbers of users, and there was no mechanism to keep two investigators from attempting to work simultaneously on the same case. Investigation of these issues indicated that a major rearchitecting of the system would be required to adequately address these problems. By this time, the bulk of the originally budgeted time and resources had already been expended. It was estimated that at least this much again would be needed to complete the project due to the rearchitecting required. The business community lost confidence that the IT team could actually pull this off, and the project was canceled.

Lessons Learned: Nonfunctional requirements must be taken into account from the very beginning when designing a system. The cost of retrofitting these requirements onto an existing design can easily exceed the initial development cost. To avoid such situations, it is imperative that significant nonfunctional requirements be identified and accommodated in the earliest stages of architecture and design.

Summary

Solving difficult technical problems does not make a project successful. In order to be successful, a project must deliver measurable business benefits under real business conditions. To deliver these benefits, the business process changes required to achieve these benefits and the circumstances under which those business processes are supposed to execute must be clearly understood. Only then can a system be built that is capable of delivering the expected benefits.

The two case studies examined here illustrate what can occur when the expected benefits, required business process changes, and full execution circumstances are not properly understood. In the first case study, not only were the changes to business process undefined but the expected business benefit was undefined as well. Absent this information, it is not surprising that the project delivered a system that the business community did not view as beneficial and refused to support further. Both the business and IT communities must share the blame here. The business community was remiss in not identifying the benefit it expected from the investment and in not determining the business process changes needed to realize that benefit. The IT community was remiss in not insisting on this level of direction before engaging in the project.

The second case study illustrates what can happen when an architecture is defined without considering key requirements. This is not to imply that every requirement has to be satisfied in the first release of a system. However, any requirement that is liable to present a challenge to the architecture must be considered when the architecture is first conceived. If this is done, versions of the system with partial functionality can then be built with full confidence that when it comes time to implement the difficult requirements, they can be gracefully accommodated.

Key Systems Design Questions

1. What measurable business benefit do you expect from the project?
2. What business process changes will be required to achieve the benefit?
3. Which requirements will present a challenge to the architecture?

Chapter 4

SOA: More Than Services

Any discussion of service-oriented architectures (SOAs) has to begin by discussing the notion of a service. But you need to go beyond the concept of services and the technologies employed. Services are important because they are a means of achieving specific business benefits. You need to be clear about what those benefits are and equally clear about the discipline you need to impose in order to realize those benefits.

What Is a Service?

A service is a unit of functionality packaged for convenient and consistent use. Typically, this functionality consists of a body of information and a set of operations for managing this information. For example, the sales order management service depicted in Figure 4–1 manages information about sales orders. It keeps records of sales orders, both current and closed, and provides operations for manipulating those orders.

While it is important to understand what a service manages, it is equally important to understand what the service does not manage. In the case of the sales order management service, the service does not directly manage customer and product information, even though sales

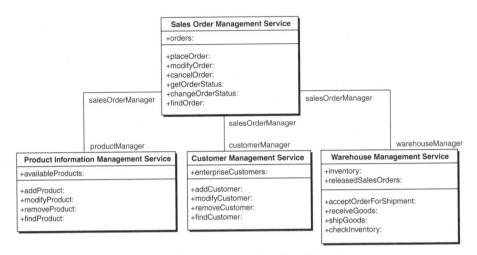

Figure 4–1: *Sales Order Management and Related Services*

orders involve information about customers and products. Instead, this service relies on other services to manage that information.

The idea of a service is to take a well-defined scope of functionality and make it readily and uniformly accessible, regardless of where the service is used. Enterprises accept orders in a variety of ways. Customers enter their orders on the web. Sales representatives enter orders from their own applications. There are business-to-business relationships in which customer systems enter their orders electronically into your systems. Despite this variety of access points, you want to implement the sales order management functionality only once and to have a single interface to this service. You don't want to duplicate either the order management logic or the interfaces. You want a single implementation with a single set of interfaces. This is the concept of a service.

The functionality provided by a service generally extends beyond the invocation of a service operation. Information underlies the service, and the operations provide the means of manipulating this information. Executing one operation affects the behavior of other operations. For example, using the `placeOrder` operation causes the service to retain information about the order. This affects the behavior of the other operations. You can neither find an order that hasn't been placed nor cancel an order that doesn't exist.

Services typically incorporate business rules as well as information. For example, most businesses will not allow you to cancel an order once it has shipped. The `cancelOrder` operation typically includes a business rule that checks to see whether the order is still in a state where it can be canceled. If the order has already shipped, the operation returns a reply indicating that the operation could not be performed, ideally containing an explanation.

A service is a complete package containing the information being managed, the operations for manipulating that information, and the business rules governing that manipulation. The business benefit from using a service is simple: The service allows you to avoid having to duplicate any of this functionality regardless of where it is employed.

Business and Infrastructure Services

A sales order management service is a business service. Business services encapsulate pieces of business functionality. They are the building blocks of business processes. However, not every service is a business service. You can derive business benefit from service-encapsulating lower-level pieces of functionality as well. A centralized exception-reporting service, for example, can be used by many applications. We call these infrastructure services.

While there are many technical similarities between business and infrastructure services, there is an important difference when it comes to validating and specifying them. By and large, infrastructure services are services provided by the IT community for use by the IT community. They encapsulate technical capabilities such as communications, messaging, user authentication and authorization, component and process monitoring, and logging and exception handling. The IT community has sufficient knowledge to evaluate proposals for these types of services. Its knowledge and experience base is broad enough to specify these services with a high degree of confidence that they will be usable in many different contexts.

The same cannot be said for business services. In most enterprises, the IT community is not in a position to validate that a proposed business service will be usable in different business circumstances. The IT community's perspective is not broad enough to specify a business service with any confidence that it will actually be reusable in different business process contexts.

To illustrate this point, consider a multinational corporation that has a variety of different business units. One unit manufactures power generation equipment, another manufactures major appliances, while a third operates a credit card business. Now consider a project team implementing a new order management system for the appliance group and wondering about making it into a service—our order management service. Does it make sense to use a common order management service across the enterprise?

The IT group can ask this question but is unlikely to have sufficient information to answer it. Someone familiar with each of the businesses might know whether it makes sense to have a single service manage the ordering of nuclear fuel, washing machines, and credit cards. In this admittedly extreme example, intuition tells you that a common order entry service would not make sense. But most real-world situations are more subtle than this, and these subtleties are primarily understood by the business side of the house. The reality is that when it comes to business services, you must have the business community actively involved in validating and specifying services.

Most Service Functionality Already Exists

It is rare to build a service from scratch. Your enterprises and their supporting information systems are ongoing works in progress. Most of the functionality you need in business processes already exists either in a custom-built legacy system or in a commercial off-the-shelf (COTS) software package. Unfortunately, that functionality is not always readily accessible in the places you want to use it.

To improve the accessibility of this functionality, you can repackage it as a service. You add a new component, often referred to as a service wrapper, that provides a service interface. The service wrapper acts as an intermediary between the service consumer and the actual provider of the functionality. Putting a service wrapper around existing functionality yields the service architecture shown in Figure 4–2.

The technology used to implement the service wrapper is often different from the technology used to implement the underlying functionality. This has a couple of implications. First, the service wrapper must be capable of employing whatever native interfaces the existing functional implementation happens to provide. This ability to use these existing interfaces becomes a selection requirement for the technology you will use to construct the wrapper. Second, because of the technology differences, it is likely that different groups will be responsible for the wrapper and the underlying functionality. This puts the organizational issues discussed in Chapter 1 squarely on the table once again.

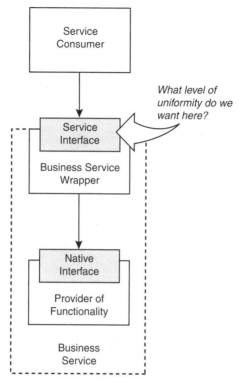

Figure 4–2: *Service Wrapping of Existing Functionality*

Creating Effective Services

On the surface, a service looks much like any other component providing functionality through a collection of interfaces. What, then, distinguishes a service from a more traditional implementation? Furthermore, what differentiates a "good" service from a "bad" service?

The answers to these questions are summed up in two words: stability and accessibility. These two qualities allow you to obtain value from using services. Stability makes a service interface an invariant in a landscape of evolving business processes and systems. This stability allows the service implementation and the service consumer to evolve independently, each without affecting the other. This keeps projects simple and facilitates the evolution of both business processes and systems.

Accessibility is the other key service property. By making the service operations readily accessible regardless of technology or location, you avoid additional development work when you need a new access to the service. You avoid the cost of developing new interfaces or, even worse, replicating the functionality.

Achieving these two qualities requires you to address seven points when designing services (or service wrappers):

1. Functional stability
2. Event support
3. Universal accessibility
4. Flexibility in implementation technology
5. Location transparency
6. Independent access control
7. Standardized message content and structure

Functional Stability

If you want your services to be points of stability in your design, the functionality that the service provides must be relatively stable. This does not mean that the functionality will never change. It means that most of the time the existing functionality will be sufficient in future projects. The benefit is that you avoid having to alter the service to support the future usages—at least most of the time.

In considering stability and change, you have to make a distinction between adding new functionality and modifying existing functionality. Modifying existing functionality is disruptive. It requires changes to the service implementation, the existing interfaces, and the users of the service. Such changes tend to be broad in scope and correspondingly complex and expensive to implement.

Additive changes, on the other hand, do not affect existing interfaces, or at least do not require changes to existing users of those interfaces. Additive changes allow you to evolve the functionality of the service without having to modify existing service clients.

In order for a service to be successful, you need to avoid (or at least minimize) the modification of existing functionality. At the same time, you must also recognize that such changes are eventually inevitable. Thus while you seek stability, you must also plan for the eventual disruptive changes.

Service Evolution

When it comes to evolving service functionality, the very success of a service can end up creating a problem. If you have many clients using the service, how you go about changing the functionality requires some thought. The obvious approach is to simultaneously change both the service and all of its clients in a single "big bang" project. Unfortunately, such projects are complex, expensive, difficult to coordinate, and risky.

The alternative to the "big bang" update is an evolutionary approach. This approach involves deploying the new version of the service while simultaneously supporting the old version. Once you deploy the new version of the service, you can migrate the service clients one at a time. Once you migrate the last client, you can retire the old version of the service. Because of the cost, complexity, and risk associated with "big bang" updates, you should always design services so that old and new versions of service operations can be simultaneously deployed. You will then be able to employ the lower-risk migration strategy.

Achieving Stability

Despite the fact that evolution will eventually be required, you want to design your services in such a way that evolution is an occasional event rather than an everyday occurrence. Accomplishing this is probably the single most challenging aspect of service design. It requires that you take out your crystal ball, look into the future, and anticipate future service needs.

The key to success in this somewhat speculative forward look lies in having the right people gazing into the future. The more senior and experienced the personnel, the better the view. If you want service stability, when projects identify candidates for services you need to get your senior people involved. They need to validate that the proposed service makes sense and specify it broadly enough that it is likely to meet future needs. Then the project team can proceed with the service implementation.

The challenge you face in doing this is both operational and organizational. Operationally, these senior people are not just sitting around waiting for the telephone to ring. If you are serious about services, you need to establish procedures whereby these people can be engaged in a timely manner, and you will need to make the servicing of such requests a priority. If project teams are not able to engage these people, schedule pressures will force the teams to guess about the services they build. The most likely outcome will be services that will require changes to support future usages—exactly what you are trying to avoid. All of the benefits will be lost.

There is an organizational aspect to this as well. While senior IT personnel are in a position to evaluate and specify infrastructure services, you will need to engage business people—and senior ones at that—to evaluate business service proposals. This is likely to be both an organizational and a procedural challenge. You probably don't have procedures for involving business folks after the requirements phase is complete. Yet this involvement is essential if you want business services to work. You need to determine how you are going to make this happen if you want to be successful with business services.

Event Support

When you think of a service, you might tend to think of a service provider passively waiting for and responding to service requests—requests for particular operations to be performed. In the earlier example, you probably think about the sales order management service responding to a `placeOrder` request. If you examine the communications involved in request-reply exchanges, you will see that each message represents either a request for an operation to be performed or a reply to such a request.

But there is another mode in which services can operate. A service can be designed to notify interested parties that specific events have occurred. For example, stock market trading services routinely send out notifications when trades occur. The well-known stock market ticker is a display of these notifications. The communications involved here are announcements of events that have occurred, not requests or replies.

Even request-reply operations come in a couple of flavors. In one variation, the requestor waits for the reply after sending the request. This is referred to as a synchronous request-reply. In the other variation, the requestor does not wait around for the reply but expects it to be sent later. This is referred to as an asynchronous request-reply. Note that the sending of the reply here is essentially an event notification announcing the completion of the request.

Real-world business processes require a mixture of these interaction styles. When you go online to order a book, it is not a synchronous request-reply interaction. The book does not arrive while you are sitting at the keyboard (unless you have ordered an electronic book). While you get an immediate acknowledgment of your order, the remainder of the process involves asynchronous interactions and event notifications. The order entry system tells the warehouse management service to ship the book but does not receive a response until after the book ships. This is an asynchronous request-reply. Meanwhile, you get e-mails about the status of your book order. These are notifications.

Because all of these interaction styles are a natural part of your business processes, you want to ensure that your service infrastructure is capable of supporting all of these interaction styles. It is not at all unusual for the same service to have different interaction styles for different operations. Just look at the stock market trading service. It has request-reply interactions for the operations used to execute trades, but it also has notification operations to inform other parties that these trades have occurred. You need full support for all interaction styles.

Universal Accessibility

You want your services to be readily accessible wherever they are needed. This means that you need access from mainframe, UNIX, Linux, and Windows environments and in a variety of programming languages. To get the payback for services, you need to be able to use the service regardless of the programming language or computing environment. In order to accomplish this, you need to provide your services using an access technology that is available in all of these environments.

An access technology meeting this requirement has two components: a universally accessible communications transport and a platform-independent content representation technology. Developing such capabilities is not trivial—not something you want your organization to do on its own. For this reason, it is good practice to choose transports and representation technologies that are industry standards. Commonly used transports are Hypertext Transport Protocol (HTTP) and Java Messaging Service (JMS), but other transports such as e-mail can be used as well. eXtensible Markup Language (XML) is commonly used as a content representation technology. Embracing these technology standards not only avoids the development and maintenance costs associated with the development of proprietary in-house standards but also allows you to share in a much more extensive engineering effort than your own staff could likely afford to execute.

These standard transport and data representation technologies will handle the bulk of your services needs, but there may be some requirements for which they are not appropriate. Streaming media such as audio and video will likely require alternate transports and data representations. It may be appropriate to use alternate transports and content representations for the bulk transfer of massive data sets as well.

Each transport and content representation that you employ in your enterprise requires an investment in technology and training as well as an initial decrease in productivity as your people climb the learning curve associated with any new technology. For efficiency, you want to manage and minimize the number of transports used in your enterprise. You should establish and enforce enterprise standards for transport and content representation technologies. If you don't, you will end up with a mixture of transports and representations that is little better than today's hodgepodge of point-to-point interfaces—the very mess that you are trying to get away from.

However, we should not expect to arrive at a single standard for either transport or data representation, even for the same service and the same operation. There are legitimate reasons (discussed in the companion volume for this book, *SOA in Practice: Implementing Total Architecture*) for supporting the use of both HTTP and JMS as service transports. You will typically find that HTTP is best for external services (those your business partners and customers use), while JMS is best for internal services (those your applications provide for one another). Similarly, while there are advantages to using XML as an information representation technology, there are valid reasons for using other representations as well—particularly when massive data sets are involved. Your goal, therefore, should be to minimize the number of technologies in use, but don't necessarily expect to have a single technology for each purpose.

Flexibility in Implementation Technology

As already noted, the bulk of the functionality needed to operate your enterprise already exists in a variety of applications. Furthermore, much of this functionality is accessible through existing interfaces. The problem is that these interfaces are written using technologies that are not universally accessible. In other words, they are not services.

For these applications, you are faced with a choice. Either you can modify the application to use your chosen service access technologies, or you can introduce an intermediary component, a service wrapper, as illustrated earlier in Figure 4–2. When the existing application is a piece of commercial software or a fragile piece of legacy code, you often do not have much choice in this matter. Modifying the application is not an option—you must use the service wrapper approach.

When you choose the service wrapper approach, make sure that the technology you select to implement the wrapper can interact with all of the different platforms and programming languages in which your applications are written. You want to standardize on a wrapper technology that is capable of accessing any technology, old or new, that you might find in your enterprise. Be careful not to fall into the trap of thinking that you need to access only the technologies you presently have or plan to use. A single merger or acquisition can render that assumption false. Like it or not, you will have to work with whatever technology comes with the deal.

Location Transparency

The service interface introduces a point of stability between the service provider and the service consumer. The functional stability discussed earlier is one essential aspect of this. It isolates each participant from internal design changes in the other. But service requests need to be somehow physically directed from the service consumer to the service provider. If the service requests are sent directly to the service provider, this creates a physical dependency between the two: The service consumer must know the physical location of the service provider in order to direct the request (Figure 4–3).

Stability is lost when service consumers must know about the physical location of service providers. Changing the location of the service provider requires changing the configuration of the service consumer. While some level of stability is achievable at the network level with virtual hostnames and virtual IP addresses, these approaches are limited in their flexibility, particularly across different physical sites.

For this reason, it is a common services practice to introduce a level of indirection in directing the communications (Figure 4–4). With indirection, the service consumer directs requests to an abstract destination

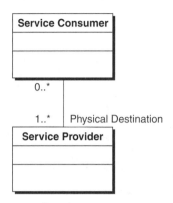

Figure 4–3: *Direct Access to Services*

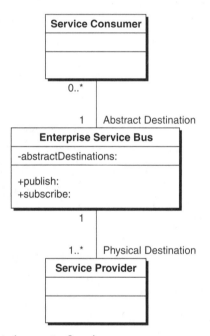

Figure 4–4: *Indirect Access to Services*

that is just a name. The destination name indicates the intent of the communication. In the sales order example, the destination might be named `SalesOrderService.placeOrder`.

Despite the use of destination names, communications must still be physically directed somewhere. In fact, they are directed to an inter-mediary commonly referred to as an enterprise service bus (ESB). The

ESB accepts the request on behalf of the service provider and then forwards the request to the service provider. Similarly, the ESB accepts the response from the service provider and forwards it back to the service consumer. The ESB is itself a service: a service communications delivery service! It is a good example of an infrastructure service.

By using an ESB, neither the service consumer nor the service provider needs to know about the physical location of the other participant. You attain location independence and achieve another level of stability at the interface. As a result, you are now free to alter the deployment of participants without worrying about changing the configurations of other participants.

Routing and the Distributed ESB

I've been referring to the ESB as if it were a single entity, but the ESB is singular only in a logical sense. When an enterprise has computing resources at more than one physical location, you need to provide ESB services at each location. Unless you do this, you will again introduce location dependencies into the participants (this time, dependencies on the ESB location). Furthermore, if there are communications problems between locations, you will still want to be able to use the ESB services to support communications within each location.

To avoid ESB location dependencies and provide ESB services at each site regardless of long-haul communications problems, you need an ESB component at each location. Figure 4–5 illustrates this, showing a service consumer residing at one physical location and a service provider residing at another. Each participant uses the services of its local ESB component. These ESB components then interact with each other, as necessary, to route the request to the service provider and route the reply back to the service consumer.

The use of a local ESB component does not, by itself, completely eliminate location dependencies. To achieve this, you need to use mechanisms such as virtual IP addresses and virtual hostnames so that the location of the local ESB component can be changed (within a physical site) without changing the configuration of the service providers and service consumers.

Routing can get much more complicated. The example shown in Figure 4–5 is the simplest form of routing: a request going from a single service consumer to a single service provider. Here the ESB is essentially mapping a logical destination to a single physical service provider. The

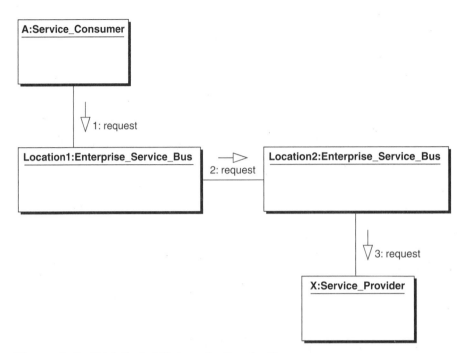

Figure 4–5: *Distributed Enterprise Service Bus*

only information needed is a mapping between the abstract destination name and the physical location (known only to the ESB) of the service provider.

Real-world applications very often require more complex routing and correspondingly more information to implement the routing. For example, when the volume of service requests is higher than a single service provider can handle, the ESB must divide the requests between two or more service providers.

However, this load distribution may not be as simple as just randomly assigning requests to service providers. Some service operations must be executed in the exact sequence that they were requested. Consider the operations on a bank account. Someone makes a deposit and then transfers funds to pay a bill. For correct results, it is important to complete the deposit before transferring the funds. If you randomly assign the deposit operation to one service provider and the debit operation to another, there is no longer any guarantee that the deposit will be completed before the debit occurs.

The upshot of this is that load distribution often requires business rules to manage such situations. The ESB must be capable of not only executing such rules but also accessing the information used by the rules. Some of this information may be in the request itself. Other information may be reference data. In the bank account example, the key piece of information is the identifier of the bank account, and the business rule is that operations performed on a given account must be performed in the sequence in which they were initiated. The ESB must be able to access this information in the request as well as apply the business rule.

More complex routing may require access to reference information. Consider the international bank example shown in Figure 4–6. Accounts for North American customers are maintained in one system, while accounts for European customers are maintained in another. When a European customer comes into a North American branch of the bank, the account requests need to be routed to the European service provider. If you want all account accesses to be uniform (the goal of services), the ESB must retrieve the account identifier from the request and determine which service provider will service the request.

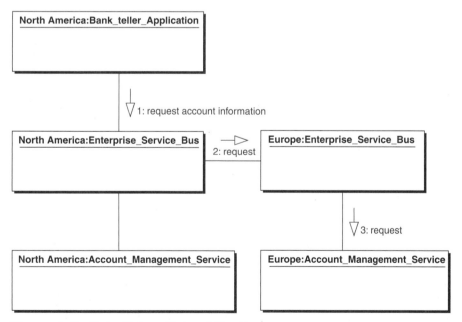

Figure 4–6: *Data-Driven Request Routing*

In order to determine which service provider to use, the ESB needs some reference data associating account identifiers with service providers, as well as the locations of the service providers. The ESB needs to be able to access the account identifier in the request, and it needs to be able to access reference information indicating which blocks of accounts are affiliated with which service providers. The ESB must also use the rules for applying this information in routing the messages. Note that the use of reference information and rules provides flexibility in which service provider is managing which accounts.

Independent Access Control

With a service-oriented architecture, your enterprise conducts its business through its services, both internally and externally. Through these services, you accept sales orders, place orders for goods, and make payments. But you have to be careful; you can't just let anybody invoke these operations! While you have made these operations readily accessible by making them into services, you now have to control who has access to these services. You may also need to limit access to the information contained in the messages being passed. These are access control requirements.

The Elements of Access Control

If you are going to control access to a service operation, the first thing to do is understand who is attempting to access the service. Typically the party attempting access will supply some form of identifying credentials such as a user ID/password combination or a security certificate. You need to validate that the credentials supplied are legitimate. This operation is generally referred to as *authentication*.

The second thing to do is check to see whether the holder of these credentials is authorized to access the particular operation being requested. For this, you need some reference information. Someone needs to have established which credentials have permission to access which operations. With this reference information in hand, *authorization* checks to see whether the credentials allow access to the operation.

The third thing to do is limit access to the sensitive data in the communications. This is generally accomplished by encrypting the sensitive data while it is being communicated and then decrypting it at the receiving end. These *encryption* activities involve encryption keys that are needed to access the sensitive data.

Other access control operations may also be required. These include the service consumer validating the identity of the service provider, maintaining audit logs of which party accessed which services, and maintaining nonrepudiation records—records of access whose validity cannot be denied.

Placement of Access Control Services

Authentication, authorization, encryption, and other such operations can all be looked on as operations of an access control service. The purpose is not to exhaustively enumerate and explore what these access control operations are but rather to ask, "Who should be providing these services: the service provider or the ESB?"

Historically, these access control responsibilities have been split in an ad hoc manner between the network infrastructure and the application providing the service whose access is being controlled. Network capabilities are very limited, particularly in checking authorization at the individual operation level. These limitations historically forced the application itself to do operation-level access control. This presents another stability challenge.

Placing operation-level access control in the application not only complicates the application design but also forces application changes when access control policies change. The problem this presents is that access control is rapidly evolving. Increasing concerns around security are forcing rapid changes in authentication, authorization, and encryption policies and technologies. In most organizations, these policies and technologies are changing more rapidly than the functionality of the service operations themselves. Leaving access control in the applications requires changes to each and every application every time the access control approach changes. To facilitate the evolution of access control technologies and policies, it is prudent to remove access control from the functional application and move it into the ESB.

Standardized Message Content and Structure

The service communications carry two types of information: information directly related to the operation and auxiliary information about the participants. For example, an invocation of the `placeOrder` operation must include information about what is being ordered. However, access control may also require additional information such as the credentials of the requesting party (if they are not already present as part of the operation's data).

It is beneficial to standardize the top-level structure of service communications. Furthermore, since virtually every service communication will require both types of information, it is beneficial to standardize the separation of these two information types. A widely used standard for this purpose is the W3C SOAP Envelope.[1] This standard defines the top-level structure of service communications, placing operation-specific information into a region known as the body, and auxiliary information into a region known as the header.

Beyond standardizing the top-level structure of the message, you can realize additional benefits by standardizing the representations of operation-specific information. Information about customers and orders, for example, will appear in many different operations on many different services. Establishing well-engineered standardized representations for these concepts and their relationships will reduce development time and improve quality.

There is added benefit in standardizing the structure of the auxiliary information as well. A family of web services standards (known as the WS-* family) standardizes the structure of information in the SOAP header. WS-Policy, WS-Security, and WS-SecurityPolicy standardize the representations of information related to usage policy and access control. But you have to recognize that this family of standards is a work in progress. Some standards, such as those defining XML, SOAP message structures, WS-Policy, WS-Security, and WS-SecurityPolicy, are mature and can be immediately employed. Others are still in development.

These evolving standards create a good news/bad news situation for your enterprise. The good news is that the WS-* family of standards is modular. The implementations of current standards, the structure of the SOAP message body, and the structure of the header portions of the messages related to the standards already in use will not be impacted by the later adoption of newly matured standards. The bad news is that in the meantime, your enterprise must find interim working solutions for the design problems that these emerging standards will eventually address.

---

1. The complete specification for the SOAP protocol can be found at the web site of the World Wide Web Consortium (W3C) at www.w3.org/TR/soap/.

It is in your best interest to adopt these industry standards wherever they are mature, applicable, and appropriate. A lot of engineering effort has gone into the development of these standards—far more than your enterprise could warrant investing in the development of its own proprietary standard for accomplishing the same end. It is simply not cost-effective to try to develop your own alternative standards.

The real challenge lies in addressing the functional areas for which the standards are not yet mature. If you need to implement short-term solutions, you should keep one eye on the emerging standard. In the long run, the finalized version of this standard will likely be your preferred solution. As such, your intermediate solution should be implemented in such a way that there is a straightforward evolutionary path to the new standard.

You also have to realize that many of these standards require some supporting infrastructure. For example, WS-Policy, WS-Security, and WS-SecurityPolicy allow you to specify the authentication, authorization, and encryption required for a particular operation, but they do not provide the mechanisms by which the credentials are authenticated, the access authorization is checked, or the message content is encrypted and decrypted. You must make an infrastructure investment in order to employ these standards.

Where Do Services Make Sense?

Addressing the challenges related to services requires real work. Despite the availability of a variety of standards and technological aids for implementing services, the actual implementation of a service still requires more work than simply implementing the required functionality. And, in addition to this extra design work, runtime overhead is involved in executing services. For these reasons, you don't want to arbitrarily turn every piece of functionality into a service. Not every interface should automatically become a service operation—it just doesn't make good sense on either a business or a technical level.

So where do services make sense? Well, first there is a basic technical consideration based on performance. When you create a service, you are placing some unit of functionality in a component (the service) that is separate from the user of the functionality. The user must then communicate with the service in order to gain access to the functionality, and there is overhead involved in this communication. For this separation to make sense, the amount of work being done by the service must be large enough that the extra time and work involved in the communication itself is negligible by comparison.

For example, you wouldn't turn arithmetic operations into a service. Despite the fact that addition, subtraction, and other mathematical functions are very widely used, the communications overhead would likely be much greater than the work involved in performing the operation itself. Imagine what the performance impact would be on an accounting system if every arithmetic operation it used required a round-trip communication with a mathematics service!

It is important to bear in mind that there are other mechanisms for sharing functionality beyond making it available as a service. Code libraries, for example, are the most common mechanism for sharing mathematical functions. Admittedly, you will need to provide different versions of these libraries for use with different programming languages, and this involves extra development effort, but it really is the only practical way to share such low-level functionality.

But let's assume now that the work involved in each operation is sufficiently large that it makes sense to consider it as a service. At this point, you find that business-level economic considerations become the deciding factor. Services make business sense when one or more of the following conditions exists.

1. *The functionality of the service will be used by two or more clients.* The justification for the service is that a single interface will support more than one client. A separate interface will not have to be developed for each client. A single interface also makes it easier to implement a single set of business rules for managing the service.

2. *The functionality of the service is actually provided by two or more applications.* This is often the consequence of merger and acquisition activity. Providing a single service hides the multiple providers from the service clients. Clients no longer have to worry about which application to use and how to accommodate the differences in the application interfaces. The logic for deciding which to use and adapting to the differences becomes part of the service itself.

3. *The service implementation is evolving, while the functionality it provides remains relatively stable.* An abstracted service interface becomes a point of stability, isolating the service clients from the internal changes to the service. Changes made to either the service provider or the service consumer will not affect the other participant.

Once you have passed this second litmus test, you have a service candidate that makes sense both in terms of its granularity and from an economic perspective. Now you need to ask yourself whether it will actually work as a service. Given the different potential usages for the service, you have to ask yourself a number of additional questions.

1. *Is it simple?* Can the purpose of the service be stated simply and clearly? Is the role that it will play in the larger business process obvious? Potential users of the service will have to understand its intended purpose to decide whether the service is applicable to their needs. If the purpose of the service is not clearly stated, potential users are likely to either draw the wrong conclusion or not even bother learning enough about the service to understand its purpose. This thinking about simplicity extends to the individual operations of the service.

2. *Do the operations fit the intended usages cleanly?* If the different usages actually require different behavior, and particularly if the service client has to provide hints in the form of parameter values to tell the operation what kind of behavior is required, you may actually be complicating things by trying to force these differing usages into a common operation.

3. *Is the invocation of the operation the same for all usages?* Do some usages require responses, while others do not? Are some request-reply usages synchronous, while others are asynchronous? Dissimilarity here may make it inappropriate to attempt a common operation.

4. *Are the milestones (answers to service status questions) clearly defined?* Are they the same for each usage?

5. *Are the key performance indicators (KPIs) and service-level requirements the same for each usage?* One usage may provide batches of 1,000 items but not require a response until the next day, while another may have a single item but require an immediate real-time response.

6. *Are the audit and tracking requirements the same?* One utilization context may require a log of who used the service, while another does not. If there are differences of this sort, is there a practical way to determine which actions should be taken?

7. *Are the fault tolerance and high-availability requirements the same?* An interactive use of the service may require the entire service to be highly available, while a batch use of the same service (with results returned asynchronously) may require only that the

interface be highly available. Making a common service will require that the service satisfy the most stringent requirements, regardless of the actual utilization.

If the answers to all of these questions are yes, you have a good candidate for a service. Note that you will need a fair amount of information about the potential usages before you will be able to answer these questions. You must get the right people involved and make an investment in considering these questions in order to get accurate answers. However, if you do not make this investment, you are likely to make much larger investments in building services that will never provide solid investment returns.

The Economic Realities of Services

When you decide to implement functionality as a service, you need to face some economic realities. First, and foremost, it costs more to create a service than it does to implement the functionality in a conventional way. Services require extra effort at design time to ensure their reuse. They require better documentation so that people can understand their intended usage and employ them appropriately. It does not make sense to build a service unless you can provide a business motivation for this extra investment. You will find this business motivation in two areas: IT cost reduction and business agility.

If you have identified multiple clients, multiple service providers, or rapidly evolving participants, there is an economic justification for the extra work in the form of IT cost reduction. To justify the service, you have to convince yourself that the additional costs associated with creating the service will be more than made up for by eliminating the future costs of modifying either the service provider or the service consumer.

Despite the opportunity for cost reduction, you have to realize that this cost reduction will most likely occur at some point in the future. If the service is used only once in the project in which it is created, this first project will not realize any cost savings. In fact, it will incur a cost penalty, as the implementation of the functionality as a service will cost more than a bare-bones nonservice implementation.

Because the project creating the service does not realize a benefit itself, the creation of services requires a level of organizational discipline that goes beyond the scope of a single project. The beneficiary that finally realizes the cost reduction (the second user of the service) may, in fact, be in a different organization than the one that first created and used the service.

So how do you deal with this misalignment of costs and benefits? A number of companies have successfully employed the following strategy. First, establish a policy that functionality that makes sense as a service should be implemented as a service. Second, scope each project so that it returns sufficient business value to more than justify the cost of creating the service. In other words, each project must make business sense on its own, regardless of whether or not it creates services. This strategy will allow a sustained investment in the development of services while providing real business value from every project.

A sustained investment in services will eventually give you another, potentially much larger, return on the services investment: improved enterprise agility. Once your enterprise has built up a portfolio of services, it can significantly reduce the time it takes to implement new projects. Such reductions enable your enterprise to respond to changing market conditions faster than your competitors. This type of competitive agility can yield returns on investments that make the savings from IT cost reductions pale by comparison.

Summary

Services are not about technology. Services are a means of reducing IT costs and accelerating the pace of business process evolution. In order to achieve those goals, you have to keep the big picture in focus. You have to understand the various business processes into which the services are expected to fit and understand them well enough to stabilize the service interfaces. You won't get either benefit unless these service interfaces remain relatively stable as business processes evolve.

The only way to gain stability in these service interfaces is to ensure that your senior people are involved in their justification and specification. You need their experience and insight, as they are the only people who can look at a proposed service and decide whether it makes sense in your enterprise. Furthermore, they are the only ones who can define those stable interfaces—interfaces that will stand the test of time as business processes evolve.

You have to make sure that you don't go overboard with services as well. Implementing a service costs more than implementing the same functionality in a more traditional way. That extra cost makes sense only when the stability of the service interface reduces the cost of subsequent changes to the service provider and service consumer. Functionality should be implemented as a service only when specific benefits from stabilizing that particular interface can be identified.

Despite your best efforts, however, you will never build the perfect service. You should be happy if the majority of service changes simply add new functionality without modifying the existing functionality. But changes will inevitably be required. At that point, both the service providers and the service consumers will require modification. You don't want to force yourself into a "big bang" simultaneous update of all the involved participants. You want to design your services so that you can codeploy both old and new versions of the service and then migrate the service consumers a few at a time.

Remember, services are an investment. Good investments have measurable returns. You want to apply these business principles to your services. Each service should be justified in terms of its potential benefits. Then, and only then, should an investment be made in defining stable interfaces and implementing the service.

Key SOA Questions

1. What is the scope of the service? What information does it manage? What operations does it provide for managing that information? What information does it reference but not manage?

2. What business processes does the service support? What throughput, response time, and availability requirements does each business process usage place on the service?

3. What process do you use to justify, validate, and specify services?

4. What criteria do you use when justifying and validating services? Do you require the demonstration of interface reuse? Do you require that the functional and performance requirements of these usages be determined?

5. Are senior, experienced people involved in service justification and specification? What is the process for getting them involved in a timely manner?

6. Does your service infrastructure:

   a. Support asynchronous events (announcements) as well as requests?

   b. Enable access to services from all the major technology platforms?

   c. Enable the use of existing functionality on all major technology platforms?

   d. Enable the routing of service requests between physical locations?

   e. Separate access control and routing from the implementation of the underlying functionality so that they can be changed independently?

7. Have you standardized the format of your service communications? Is the format an industry standard or one developed in-house?

8. Have you standardized the representations of information in your service communications?

Suggested Reading

Cabrera, Luis Felipe, and Chris Kurt. 2005. *Web Services Architecture and Its Specifications: Essentials for Understanding WS-**. Redmond, WA: Microsoft Press.

World Wide Web Consortium. "Latest SOAP Versions." www.w3.org/TR/soap/.

Chapter 5

Keys to SOA Success

The case studies in Chapters 2 and 3 illustrate the kinds of problems that can arise when systems become disconnected from their business purpose and, by extension, from the business processes they are intended to support. This chapter takes a deeper look at the relationship between systems and business processes. You will see that as business processes become increasingly reliant on systems, the design of the business processes and the design of the systems become so interdependent that the design of one cannot be addressed without considering the design of other. This interdependency then impacts how to think about the design process and systems architecture.

What Makes a Project Good?

Why do you build information systems? The answer seems obvious on the surface: to benefit the enterprise. However, this answer is too vague to be of practical use. It does not provide any specifics to guide development processes toward delivering that benefit. It provides neither a standard against which you can measure the "goodness" of a system nor any means of deciding whether one approach is better or worse than another. Such a vague answer does not provide enough information to determine whether the system has managed to improve the enterprise at all! You need specifics.

When a business charters a project, there are expectations about the benefits that the project will produce. In order to effectively guide the project, you need to understand specifically what those expected benefits are, and you need to be able to quantify them. Yes, you need to know that the purpose of the project is to enable the enterprise to handle more business with the same staff. But you also need to know, for example, that "more" means the business volume must increase by at least 50% without increasing staff and that the results must be operational within 12 months.

Quantifying these benefits establishes objective criteria for determining project success. If the project goal is to enable a 50% increase in volume without increasing staff, and the business is able to achieve only a 5% increase, the project has not succeeded. The establishment of criteria also raises the question as to how the improvement will be measured. This question will in turn generate requirements for the new business processes and systems to capture the data necessary to support this measurement. Note that this success can be measured only after the new business processes and systems have been deployed. The business doesn't benefit from the deployment—the business benefits from the usage of the new business processes and systems!

Quantifying the benefits also provides a basis for deciding whether a proposed design can actually deliver the expected benefits. In other words, if you cannot make a reasonable case that a proposed design will enable a 50% increase in volume without increasing staff, that design is not acceptable. Making a credible argument also requires talking about the business processes and the changes in them that will enable the enterprise to achieve the expected benefits. Without a quantified benefit, no amount of discussion about business processes will enable you to decide whether or not a given design will achieve that benefit.

In the same vein, quantifying benefits also provides a yardstick for comparing alternative business process and systems designs in terms of their ability to provide the expected benefits. If one alternative will be able to provide a 55% increase and another a 65% increase, the latter alternative would appear to be better in its ability to achieve the benefit. Without a quantifiable benefit, such comparisons would be difficult to make.

While on this topic, I should acknowledge an unpleasant fact of life about business process and system designs: Not every design actually provides benefit! Just because you have put new systems in place does not necessarily mean that the world as a whole has gotten better. In fact, improving a small portion of a business process may make the overall process worse.

As an example, chances are that you have been the victim of bad telephone answering system design. Such systems provide benefit by requiring fewer people to answer the phones, but if the customer experience worsens, the business will lose customers. Thus, in evaluating the benefits of a system, you must take into consideration the full business process and all of its stakeholders—all of the parties who are interested in the system—and the impact the system will have on each.

The Role of Cost and Schedule Budgets

Benefits are not free. Realizing a benefit requires an investment. When you charter a project, you have expectations not only about the benefits but also about what the costs will be and how long the project will take. In chartering the project, you have made a judgment that the expected benefits warrant this level of investment.

Quantifying the anticipated cost and project duration is as important to governing the project as quantifying the expected benefits. Such quantifications provide further criteria for deciding whether a design is acceptable. The overall project success question now becomes: Can the benefit be provided within the cost and schedule guidelines? This quantification also provides another metric for determining the relative merits of alternative designs. If two designs provide the same benefit, but one does so at a significantly lower cost or shorter time to complete, that design is better in this regard.

The technical community is often uncomfortable with such cost and time-frame guidelines. They are viewed with skepticism as unfounded "guesstimates" of what it will take to achieve the expected benefits. After all, how can you estimate the cost and schedule for doing something when the requirements have not even been defined?

Such thinking reflects a fundamental misunderstanding about what these cost and schedule guidelines represent. These guidelines are not an estimate of what it will take to get the job done. Rather, they are a business statement that this level of investment would be warranted by the expected benefits. As such, these cost and schedule constraints need to be viewed as a challenge to the design team: Can the design team provide this benefit within the given cost and schedule guidelines?

The Project Prime Objective

Now that you understand the role of cost and schedule guidelines, a charter for the project begins to emerge: Deliver the expected benefits within the cost and schedule guidelines. However, this formulation contains an inappropriate assumption, one that contains risk for the enterprise. This assumption is that it is possible to attain the expected level of benefit within those cost and schedule guidelines. While this assumption may be appropriate for simple changes, it becomes increasingly inappropriate as the project becomes more ambitious, expecting substantial benefits with correspondingly expansive cost and schedule guidelines.

When you launch a project, you must make some level of assumption. But you *can* mitigate the risk by focusing the project initially on specifically determining whether the expected benefits can be achieved within those cost and schedule guidelines. The goal is to make this determination as quickly as possible with as little resource expenditure as possible. The project charter now becomes the ***project prime objective****: Determine whether the expected benefits are attainable within the cost and schedule guidelines; if they are, deliver the benefits within those guidelines.*

Making a feasibility assessment is usually not a singular event in the project lifecycle. It tends to be an ongoing process as the understanding of the problem domain unfolds and the possible solutions are explored. However, you can organize the work to reach early conclusions. Focus the early stages on identifying the most complex and challenging business processes, defining the operational concept for how their modification will produce the expected benefits, determining that there is at least one feasible architecture, and determining that this architecture can be built within the cost and schedule guidelines. If you can't find a satisfactory solution here, there is little point in proceeding further. Once you have convinced yourself that you can address the most complicated aspects within the cost and schedule guidelines, you have significantly reduced the risks. This approach is embodied in the Total Architecture Synthesis (TAS) methodology that I will describe in Chapter 9.

Conducting a project with an explicit feasibility assessment has project governance implications. The oversight team must be aware of the possibility that the cost and schedule guidelines for the project may not turn out to be realistic. The governance process must provide procedural mechanisms for the project to report its feasibility findings, and the oversight team must be prepared to adjust the project charter accordingly. To minimize the risks to the enterprise, the governance process must also encourage early reporting on feasibility since early notification provides maximum flexibility for the enterprise.

Should a project turn out to be infeasible, if most of the budgeted money remains unspent and most of the budgeted time still remains, there are many options available. The project can be redefined, adjusting the expected benefits and/or renegotiating the cost and schedule guidelines. If an acceptable cost/benefit combination cannot be found, the remaining resources can be applied toward achieving other benefits. Late identification of infeasible projects, after most of the time and money have been expended, leaves few options. It also puts the oversight team in the awkward position of not being able to fulfill the promises it made to the enterprise.

The Good Project

If you could put a quality meter on a project to report on its benefit to the enterprise, you might end up with something that looks like Figure 5–1. In this hypothetical measurement, a good project is one that actually delivers a quantifiable benefit to the enterprise and does so within the cost and schedule guidelines. Early in the project, the reading on this meter would be very inaccurate and fuzzy, reflecting the uncertainties involved. As the project progresses, the requirements become clearer, the design unfolds, and the reading becomes clearer and more accurate. The final reading, the ultimately accurate one, cannot be taken until the revised business processes and systems have been deployed and the business is actively using them. Only then will you know the final cost and whether you have realized the expected benefits.

Figure 5–1: *Evaluating the Project Impact on the Business*

The ongoing challenge to the project and oversight teams is to ensure that the meter ends up in the "good" zone.

The System Is the Process!

Early computers played no role whatsoever in the definition or management of business processes. Although the computer performed the mechanical task of computing the payroll, people decided when that payroll should be run, decided what data to use, and validated the results. The computer was just a tool for performing tasks, like a hammer. People owned the business process, determining how and when to apply the tools.

At the core of these early computer-centric business processes was a schedule of which computer jobs should be run and which related magnetic tapes, punch cards, and printouts needed to be moved around. The procedures for doing these things were carefully documented in checklists and run books to ensure that no steps were omitted. People were responsible for the quality control of the process. When things went wrong, people identified the fact that there was a problem, determined what to do as a result, and executed the recovery plan.[1]

Although these early computers did not participate in the management of business processes, they did contain the seeds of computer-aided process management. Their work was defined by a set of punch cards, each containing a command for the computer. The cards actually defined a simple process. Once a person had mounted the tapes, loaded the punch cards, and started the job (as the card deck was referred to), the computer could autonomously execute the process defined by the deck.

Executing a process, however, is very different from managing it. Managing a process requires understanding how the process is supposed to execute, monitoring its actual execution, noting any differences, and taking appropriate action. While early computers could execute a simple process, they had virtually no ability to detect and respond to errors. This was a human responsibility.

---

1. John Gall's book, *Systemantics: How Systems Work and Especially How They Fail* (1977), contains a number of humorous anecdotes of people failing to act appropriately when they observe things that are not quite what they should be.

As technology advanced, computers became capable of storing both programs and data online. The computers began to keep track of business process execution. As people interacted with computers to perform their business activities, the computer updated the business process records. The online availability of business process records now made it possible to incorporate business process status into tasks being performed by the computer—decision-making tasks. The computer became a limited participant in the management of the business process.

Over time, computers have become ever more deeply involved in business processes. Their automation of activities has greatly increased the volume of work that can be handled. It has also created a problem. High-volume automated business processes require automatic breakdown detection. Without automatic detection, it is likely that problems—and potentially a large volume of problems—will remain unrecognized and unresolved for extended periods of time. With large-scale automation comes an increased need to involve the computer in the overall management of the business process.

Positioning the computer to manage a business process requires the computer to have a great deal of information about that business process. It must have an explicit representation of the business process so that it knows what is supposed to happen. It must know the desired performance characteristics so that it can determine whether things are happening in a timely manner and at appropriate rates. This knowledge puts the computer in a position to both direct the work and monitor its execution—whether that work is being performed by the system or by people. The computer embodies the business process and becomes its manager. In a very fundamental sense, the system has become the process.

System Design and Process Design Are Inseparable

Placing a system in the role of a process manager has far-reaching implications for the way you go about designing that system. When a system is simply a tool for performing a task, all you need to understand is the task it is supposed to perform. You do not need to understand the logic for deciding when to perform the task, determining whether the task was successfully completed, or figuring out what to do if the task did not succeed. However, you need to understand all these things when the system becomes the process manager, for they all impact the system design. You need to understand all the possible variations of the business process, how to determine whether each variation is executing properly, and what corrective actions to take for each variation.

The use of computers for business process management alters the design of your business processes, as you must consider the practical limitations of what to expect a computer to do. As I later explore in Chapter 10, systems can respond only to situations they are programmed to handle. Despite this, the reality is that you can continue to expect the unexpected from your business processes. Consequently, you need to design your systems to engage people to handle these unexpected situations. Systems must, at a minimum, identify exceptional situations and bring them to the attention of people. There is an implication for the business process design as well: A human support team is required to flexibly respond to these notifications. This operational response has to be part of the basic business process design.

Of course, if you are to derive productivity benefits from automating the management of business processes, you must keep the level of human participation modest. This means that the systems must recognize and handle the commonly encountered problems. The design process must, therefore, identify these common problems and define corrective actions. Only then can the system incorporate an appropriate level of breakdown detection and handling.

The use of computers for process management also creates a chicken-and-egg design situation. While business process design determines how and when the systems will participate, the practicality of that participation cannot be determined without partially designing the systems. You must consider the practical performance limitation of the computer. The business process defines how, when, and how often the system must act during the process. To determine whether such a system can be built within the cost and schedule guidelines, it is necessary to do at least a partial design of the system. Only then will you know whether that particular business process design can provide the expected benefits within the cost and schedule guidelines.

Toward a Refined Development Methodology

Once the systems become involved in the management of business processes, you will find significant interdependencies between the design of the business process and the design of the systems. You must understand the business process in order to build the appropriate levels of monitoring, management, and breakdown detection into the systems. The business process design must reflect the computer's performance limitations and limited ability to handle unexpected situations. Finally, you can't determine the feasibility of a business process design without at least partially designing the supporting systems. You must consider the participation of the systems in the business process and the implications of that participation as you design the business process.

You can now see a clear progression for the conduct of your projects. You need a quantified understanding of the benefits that are expected and the cost and schedule constraints. You need to determine the business process modifications that will be required to attain those benefits. You need to determine whether the proposed process is feasible from an IT perspective and have at least a rough idea of the time and cost involved in building the systems. You need all of this information in order to understand whether it is possible to provide the expected benefits within the cost and schedule guidelines.

To achieve these ends, you need a model of system development that proactively addresses these issues. This development model must maintain a sharp focus on both the expected benefits and the feasibility and practicality of achieving them at every step along the way. The interdependencies between business processes and systems require an ongoing dialog between the business and IT communities, a dialog in which each provides feedback to the other regarding the feasibility and practicality of their respective designs.

As the business process architect designs the business process, the systems architect must provide feedback regarding the systems feasibility and practicality. Does an architecture even exist that can support the business process and be built within the cost and schedule guidelines? As the design progresses, the business process architect must provide feedback to the systems architect concerning the business process refinements embodied in the evolving system design. Does the refined business process still deliver the expected benefit?

The Total Architecture Synthesis methodology described in Chapter 9 provides a practical approach to the design of information systems that implements this model. However, you need to recognize that following such a model in the context of a single project is not sufficient.

Projects themselves exist within a larger ecosystem, and that ecosystem is also impacted. The project governance process reflects that ecosystem. The ecosystem determines which business problems warrant investment. It defines what the expected benefits are and defines the cost and schedule guidelines. It charters the projects and provides the resources necessary to carry them out.

Traditionally, the governance process launches projects and then expects feedback in the form of progress reports. These progress reports identify issues that need to be addressed in order to bring the project to a successful conclusion. Implicit in the traditional governance process is the assumption that the expected benefits can, indeed, be delivered within the cost and schedule guidelines. Traditional project governance is very intolerant of negative feedback regarding project feasibility. This intolerance is a major cause of what Ed Yourdon refers to as "death march" projects—projects whose realistic cost and schedule estimates deviate from expectations by more than 50% yet continue on without adjustment.[2] This intolerance creates a high-risk environment for ambitious projects, both for the project team and for the enterprise chartering the project.

What we need is a more open-minded approach to project governance, particularly with respect to ambitious projects. This approach must recognize the initial project charter for what it really is: a statement that achieving particular benefits is worth spending a certain amount of time and investing a particular sum of money. The refined approach must acknowledge that in most cases the feasibility of achieving these benefits within the guidelines has yet to be established.

This has implications for both project governance and the conduct of the project itself. The people working on project governance must actively seek feedback regarding project feasibility and be prepared to adjust the project charter accordingly. The project team itself must focus initially on the cost/benefit/feasibility aspects of the project. It must provide timely and accurate feedback on project feasibility. Of course, in order for this to work, the culture reflected in the governance process must encourage negative feedback. If you culturally shoot the messenger of bad tidings, the ability to obtain early feedback will be lost, as will the opportunity to redirect project resources.

---

2. Edward Yourdon, *Death March* (2004).

Summary

Successful projects produce real business value. Getting a project focused on producing value requires its goals to be quantifiable, and determining whether the project has been successful requires measuring the achievement of those goals. Recognizing this, you should require that your projects establish the infrastructure to make these measurements and demand the actual measurement of your business process improvements.

You charter projects with specific expectations regarding the level of effort it will take to produce your anticipated business benefits. These expectations are not always in alignment with reality. For overall enterprise efficiency, you should clearly state your expectations, and the project team should initially focus on determining whether these expectations are sufficient to achieve the business goals. You should demand timely feedback if they are not.

Combining these two notions, you can summarize your charter for the project team in the project prime objective: *Determine whether the expected benefits are attainable within the cost and schedule guidelines; if they are, deliver the benefits within those guidelines.*

Your systems are now so deeply embedded in business processes that neither can be designed independently of the other. Your systems architects, in particular, have to be careful that the changes they make to your business processes (whether accidental or intentional) actually improve those processes. To ensure good project outcomes, you should employ an integrated business process and system design methodology such as the Total Architecture Synthesis methodology described in Chapter 9.

Key Development Process Questions

1. Are you chartering projects with quantified expectations of benefits and clearly defined cost and schedule guidelines?
2. Do you have a well-defined governance milestone marking the establishment of project feasibility? Does it assess the feasibility of delivering the quantified benefits within the cost and schedule guidelines?

3. Does the enterprise culture support the timely reporting of negative feedback regarding project feasibility?

4. Does the development process call for the clear definition of the business process changes required to produce the benefits?

5. Does the development process surface and resolve inconsistencies between the business process design and the system design during the design process?

Suggested Reading

Gall, John. 1977. *Systemantics: How Systems Work and Especially How They Fail*. New York: Random House Trade.

Smith, Howard, and Peter Fingar. 2003. *IT Doesn't Matter: Business Processes Do*. Tampa, FL: Meghan-Kiffer Press.

Yourdon, Edward. 2004. *Death March, Second Edition*. Upper Saddle River, NJ: Prentice Hall.

Chapter 6

Organizing for SOA Success

The design of enterprise-scale business processes and supporting systems touches on many organizations and projects within the enterprise. The business processes themselves coordinate the work of a number of business groups, and the underlying systems coordinate the work of the applications belonging to those business groups. Each business group typically has an IT group dedicated to the care and feeding of its applications. All of these organizations must be involved in one way or another in the development of the business processes and systems.

The grouping of a business unit and its supporting IT organization is often referred to as a *silo*—a term I will use quite a bit in this chapter and beyond. Each silo typically focuses on achieving specific goals related to the business unit's function within the enterprise. Sales focuses on obtaining orders for the business and managing the cost associated with obtaining orders. Manufacturing focuses on producing product while managing production costs and meeting delivery commitments. Silos tend to be independently managed, inwardly focused, and relatively isolated from one another.

When you have projects that span two or more of these organizational silos, the number of organizations involved and their relative independence presents a major challenge. Each of the business and IT organizations involved has a natural tendency to focus narrowly on those portions of the business processes and systems that are most relevant to it.

With this silo-based focus, nobody is responsible for the big picture. Nobody is responsible for producing the expected benefits and determining what overall business process changes will be required to produce those benefits. Nobody is responsible for the overall systems design and ensuring it supports the business process. Nobody is responsible for determining whether the business process and system changes can be implemented within the cost and schedule guidelines. In short, nobody is accountable for success!

These responsibilities are vital to the success of any project that involves multiple business units, but you need to determine where these responsibilities belong in the overall organizational structure. There are many possible answers, but successful organizations generally concentrate these responsibilities into a few key roles. These roles and their organizational positioning are the focus of the next three chapters. This chapter focuses on the oversight of silo-spanning projects. Chapter 7 explores the leadership of individual projects, and Chapter 8 examines enterprise architecture leadership and concludes with a summary discussion of organizational positioning.

The Organizational Simplicity of Application Design

The exploration starts by considering the development of single applications—what are often referred to as departmental systems. A relatively small number of organizations are involved in such systems. Figure 6–1 illustrates a typical mix. The business unit manager has overall responsibility for the unit's operation. This person is the de facto owner of the business silo, which consists of the business users, the supporting information systems, and the IT organizations responsible for those information systems.

The business unit manager is typically the person who identifies the need for business improvements and charters an IT project to make those improvements. The manager sets the goals for the project and establishes the overall budget and timetable. In most cases, the business manager is also the beneficiary of the project, whose intent is to improve the business unit's operation in some fashion.

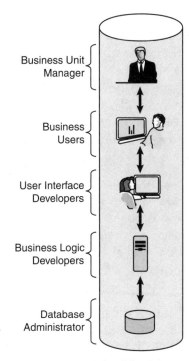

Figure 6–1: *Some Organizations Involved in Departmental Application Development*

The business users are the people who perform the daily work of the business unit. Their work generally involves some combination of manual activity and the use of supporting information systems. Supporting these information systems are one or more IT organizations focusing on the design of user interfaces, business logic, and data storage. These IT organizations usually report, either directly or with dotted-line responsibility,[1] to the business unit manager.

The development process for departmental applications, illustrated earlier in Figure 1–2, tends to be rather simple. The business unit manager identifies the need for a change and charters the project. The

---

1. In the case of dotted-line reporting, the IT manager reports directly to higher-level IT management (*solid-line* reporting) but has the responsibility of meeting the IT requirements of the business manager. This responsibility and relationship to the business manager is often formalized as the IT manager having a *dotted-line* reporting responsibility to the business manager.

project itself is structured as a series of meetings between the various groups within the silo. This works because of the relatively small number of groups involved and because the business process changes are largely confined to the silo. The business unit manager and business users sit down and agree on how the revised business process will work and how the systems will participate in that process. Often with the aid of a business analyst, they generate a set of business requirements. These business requirements are then passed to the IT organization to be turned into a working system.

System changes are usually confined to the applications belonging to the business unit. The developers sit down with the business users and develop the technical requirements for the user interface and business logic. The developers then work among themselves to understand the information used in the application and determine how their respective components will interact. Finally, the changes are implemented and tested, and the system is placed into production.

This approach to application development works reasonably well for several reasons. First, the number of groups (organizations) involved is relatively small, and their responsibilities are clear. Second, the business unit manager has direct control over the business process and indirect control (via the budget) of the overall development process. This puts the business unit manager in a position to make and enforce decisions and thus bring focus to the project. Third, the architecture and high-level design of the system remain unaltered more often than not. Even when architectural decisions must be made, their scope is modest, and the small number of IT groups involved can get together to make them. As long as there is a good working relationship between the business unit manager and the head of the silo's IT organization, any issues that arise can be readily resolved to the satisfaction of both. Every problem has a well-defined owner.

The Organizational Complexity of Distributed System Design

Life is considerably more complex when designing a distributed system. A distributed system is one that involves two or more major systems (applications) acting as peers. Each system performs its work independently of the others and typically exists to support a particular business unit in its activities. The systems do exchange information with each other as part of the business process, but none of the systems is explicitly responsible for the overall process.

Not only are there multiple silos involved, but the company often acquires new service and integration technology and creates yet another IT organization to manage that new technology. Another silo! As the number of silos grows, so does the complexity of intergroup communications required to collectively design the system. If you simply integrate two major systems, you end up with the pattern of intergroup communications shown in Figure 6–2.

What's wrong with this picture? Simply put, there's nobody in charge. In the application development scenario, the business unit manager essentially had control over the complete development process. But who is in charge in a distributed system design? Who owns the overall business process? Who establishes the goals for the project? Who can ensure the cooperation of the participants?

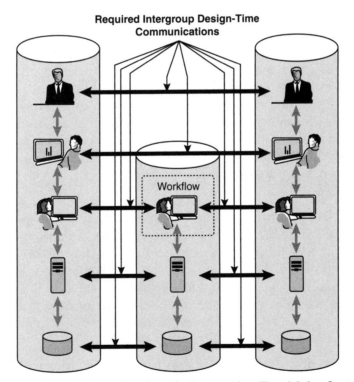

Figure 6–2: *Organizations Involved in Integrating Two Major Systems*

Organizing Multisilo Projects

In order for any project to be successful, somebody must be responsible for the overall result. The problem you run into with a multisilo project is that the silo-based organizational structure does not inherently provide a "somebody" to own this overall responsibility. To bring a results-oriented focus to these multisilo projects without completely reorganizing the silos (a practical impossibility), you need to add some overall leadership to the project.

This leadership is required in three areas: project resource management, overall business process design, and overall systems design. Adding this leadership gives us a project structure similar to the one shown in Figure 6–3. In this structure, the project manager has the overall responsibility for the project. To make this work, the project manager's responsibility must extend beyond the traditional management of technical development work. The project manager must be responsible for delivering nothing less than an improved business process that produces the expected business result.

To produce those expected benefits, someone needs to determine exactly what needs to be done at both the business process and systems levels. These are the respective responsibilities of the business process architect and the systems architect. Jointly, they are responsible for the design of the end-to-end business processes and their supporting systems. Furthermore, they are responsible for ensuring that this end-to-end design actually delivers the expected business benefits. As a team, the project manager, business process architect, and systems architect work together to ensure that the expected business benefits are delivered.

In this project structure, personnel in the individual silos perform the bulk of the work. Because of this, the business process and systems architects must determine what each of the silos needs to do in order to achieve the overall business goals. This determination goes beyond simply deciding what development work each silo will do. It extends to defining which activities each silo will be performing in the revised business process and how those business process activities will be coordinated with the activities of other silos.

Making practical determinations with respect to who will be doing what obviously requires the active participation of the silos. At the end

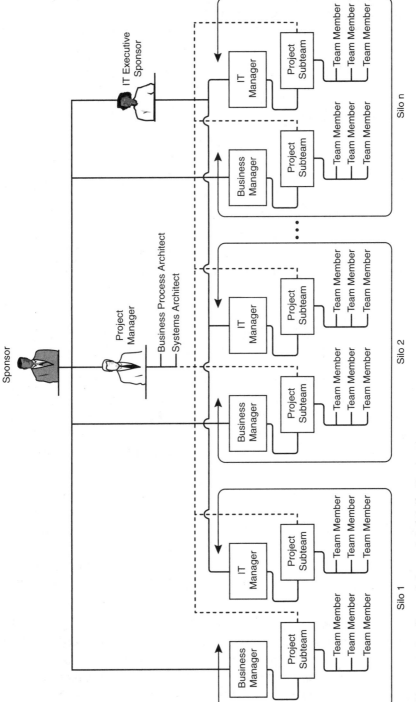

Figure 6–3: *Organizing a Multisilo Project*

of the day, individuals in the silos will be taking responsibility for their development work and their part of the business process. They need to take ownership of their individual responsibilities. Consequently, the business process and systems architects must work with these individuals and build this sense of ownership while keeping the dialog focused on achieving the overall business goals. However, for this to work, the priorities of those individuals must be aligned with the overall business priorities.

Aligning Priorities

One of the obvious challenges in a multisilo project is that the project team has no direct authority over the individuals in the silos, yet it depends on those individuals for the bulk of the work. In massive enterprise business process reengineering efforts such as enterprise resource planning (ERP), this problem is often solved by removing those individuals from the silos and reassigning them to the project team. While this approach may work for massive projects, it is impractical for smaller ones. You need an approach that works for all projects.

The industry trend toward managing and optimizing enterprise-wide business processes using service-oriented architecture is steadily increasing the number of projects that span silos. These projects are not massive, and they will not have the advantage of directly managing their own resources. You need a pragmatic approach that will enable you to assemble effective cross-silo project teams without reassigning people. The majority of the individuals working on each project will report directly to their respective silos and will have only a dotted-line reporting responsibility to the project team.

Making dotted-line reporting work requires the active support of the manager to whom the individual in the silo actually reports. After all, this direct-reporting relationship drives the individual. His or her manager sets the priorities, which should be directly reflected in performance reviews and compensation incentives. If the priorities given to the individual do not coincide with the needs of the project, the project will not succeed.

How do you ensure that these priorities are aligned? These priorities all emanate from a single source: the business executive sponsor. Who is this person? The *business executive sponsor* is that person in the organization who (a) owns the overall business processes being modified, (b) owns the project budget, (c) realizes the project benefit, and (d) has line authority *over all the personnel involved in realizing the benefit.* This is the only person who is in a position to set priorities and make balanced tradeoff decisions between budget, benefit, and organizational commitments. These responsibilities pretty much dictate that the business executive sponsor will be someone fairly high up in the organization structure. This person may, in fact, be the president, the chief operating officer (COO), or even the chief executive officer (CEO).

The business executive sponsor has line authority over the business personnel. But you must also think about aligning IT priorities. Business silos typically have their IT personnel dedicated to their silo. If these IT personnel report through the silo's business manager, the requisite prioritization will come via the business manager.

However, in many enterprises the IT personnel do not report directly through the silo's business manager: IT has its own organizational hierarchy. In this case, that hierarchy drives the priorities of the IT personnel. These priorities emanate from the IT executive sponsor. The *IT executive sponsor is that person with line authority over all of the involved IT organizations.* This is the only person in a position to adjust IT priorities as necessary to ensure the success of the project. This prioritization includes the direction of the IT budget as well as the allocation of resources. As with the business executive sponsor, the IT executive sponsor is typically positioned fairly high in the organization structure and may well be the chief information officer (CIO).

You might ask how IT priorities can become misaligned with business priorities. After all, the IT budget is rationalized at the business level and should reflect business priorities. What is approved in the budget are a number of funded initiatives, each with a business rationale. IT now focuses on executing these technical initiatives.

The technical initiatives get decomposed into projects or capital investments that are implemented by different parts of the IT organization. Unfortunately, in this decomposition, you often lose the connection between the individual IT project or investment and the business benefits expected from the overall initiative. IT personnel end up making technical decisions based on purely technical evaluations without the guiding understanding of what is truly important to the business.

You don't see the misalignment until you begin to apply the results of these IT projects and investments at the individual project level, where the emphasis is once again on solving business problems. You should view these projects as litmus tests that determine whether the IT priorities and investments are actually serving the needs of the business. In applying the results, you may come to realize that the purely technical decisions have resulted in over- or underinvestment in certain areas or in technical directions that actually run counter to the real business needs. You need to proactively communicate these priority misalignments up to the IT executive sponsor and get them resolved.

The Business Executive Sponsor–IT Executive Sponsor Relationship

In order for IT prioritization to work, the IT executive sponsor's priorities must be in alignment with those of the business executive sponsor. If the IT executive sponsor reports directly to the business executive sponsor, this is obviously not an issue. However, you often find situations in which the IT executive sponsor has a dotted-line reporting relationship to the business executive sponsor (Figure 6–4). This usually arises when the business executive sponsor is positioned below the president/COO level and the enterprise has a separate IT hierarchy that extends all the way up to the CIO.

As long as this dotted-line relationship is healthy and cooperative, the two sponsors can rationalize and align the business and IT priorities. Cross-silo projects will execute effectively. However, if this dotted-line relationship becomes strained or is nonexistent, trouble is brewing.

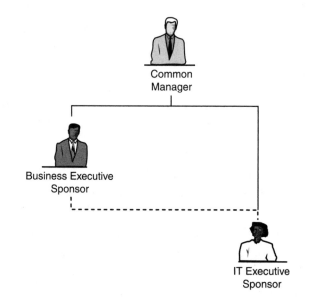

Common Manager

Business Executive Sponsor

IT Executive Sponsor

Figure 6–4: *Dotted-Line Reporting of the IT Executive Sponsor*

There is no longer any effective mechanism for bringing business and IT priorities into alignment for the project. Without such an alignment, the likelihood of a multisilo project actually producing its expected business benefits becomes vanishingly small.

The sole solution to this problem lies further up the organizational hierarchy. The only person who can remedy the situation is a manager who has line authority (directly or indirectly) over both the business and IT executive sponsors for the project. Unless that person takes action to either fix the broken dotted-line reporting relationship or directly assume the business executive sponsor role, the project is unlikely to succeed. There is no other remedy.

The Role of Incentives in Aligning Priorities

One of the most powerful tools that executive sponsors (of either flavor) have to align priorities is incentive compensation. Incentives codify the goals of the organization and keep personnel focused on achieving these goals. However, if you are not careful, this powerful tool can create a misalignment of priorities when a change in business priorities is not reflected in a corresponding adjustment to incentives.

Consider a catalog business in which the organization responsible for taking orders has incentive to keep order-processing costs as low as possible. In this same business, another organization is responsible for shipping the goods and likewise has incentive to keep warehouse management and shipment costs as low as possible. The problem is that frequent errors in order processing and fulfillment are resulting in costly returns and loss of customers. The business is under pressure to fix these problems.

Some of these order errors arise when orders are being taken, others occur when filling orders, and still others happen during the handoff between the order entry silo and the order fulfillment silo. Lowering the error rate will require additional work in each organization—and thus increase their costs. Given the current incentivization scheme, we have to ask ourselves whether either organization will be willing to increase its handling cost for an order. Probably not.

Incentive compensation is usually tied to specific performance measurements. In order for a business process improvement effort to make sense to the silo owners, the measurements driving incentives must be adjusted to reflect the new priorities. In the previous example, linking part of the incentive compensation to the measurement of error rates will help refocus everyone on reducing errors, thus reflecting enterprise priorities.

Lest you think incentives are a minor point, consider that in the 1980s the U.S. automotive manufacturing plant that had the lowest production cost per vehicle also had the industry's highest warranty defect rate. This was a direct consequence of the plant manager's compensation being based solely on vehicle production cost, with no consideration of defects. Because of incentives like this, the U.S. automotive industry lost a lot of ground to foreign manufacturers producing better-quality products.

Organizational measurements and incentive compensation drive organizational behavior. Changes in organizational goals require corresponding changes in incentive compensation and their related measurements. *Only the executive sponsors are in a position to adjust incentives.* If they are not actively adjusting incentives to match changing enterprise goals, these enterprise goals are not likely to be reached.

Systems Architecture Leadership

One of the most difficult organizational problems to overcome for cross-silo projects is a lack of effective central IT leadership. This arises either when there is no central IT organization or when that central organization lacks authority over the IT groups within the business silos. Under such circumstances, the IT organizations within the silos typically report directly to the business managers responsible for the silos (Figure 6–5).

The problem that arises with fragmented IT organizations is the lack of central leadership to guide the various IT groups toward common services and system integration approaches. In short, nobody is in a position to control the overall enterprise architecture. This places the project team in the untenable position of having to define a de facto enterprise architecture, at least for that portion related to the current project. However, such decisions impact other projects as well. If these decisions are to be consistent across projects, the project team must take into consideration the needs of other projects and future projects as well. The project team does not have the time, resources, authority, or budget to fulfill this role. The bottom line in this case is that there is no effective mechanism for defining a coherent enterprise systems architecture.

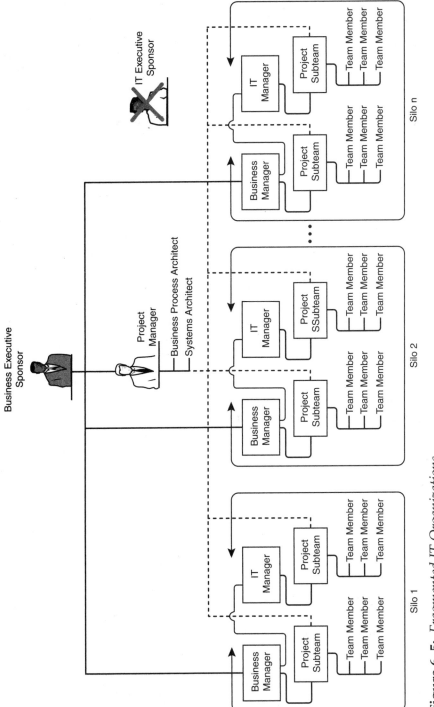

Figure 6–5: *Fragmented IT Organizations*

When the enterprise is pursuing a service-oriented architecture, a lack of enterprise IT leadership creates an impossible situation. The lack of technical consistency from project to project will result in a systems landscape that is complex to operate and expensive to maintain. In fact, it will look exactly like today's point-to-point integration nightmare, despite the use of newer SOA technologies. If you are to succeed in improving cross-silo business processes using service-oriented architectures, central leadership is essential. I will talk more about this in Chapter 8.

Project Oversight

The most critical relationship in a project is the one between the project manager and the business executive sponsor. This relationship provides the communications channel through which conflicts are resolved. However, it is unlikely that this sponsor will have sufficient time to actively oversee the project because of the sponsor's other responsibilities. Unless the project is near the top of the sponsor's priority list, the sponsor will, most likely, delegate that responsibility. The question is, to whom?

For large initiatives, project oversight responsibility is often delegated to an initiative steering committee. The project team reports directly to the steering committee, which in turn reports to the business executive sponsor. For efficiency, a member of this committee may be designated as the point of contact for day-to-day project team interactions. This person is usually empowered to make minor oversight decisions and to gather the larger committee together when more significant decisions are called for.

The actual makeup of the initiative steering committee varies greatly from enterprise to enterprise depending on the nature of the enterprise, its organizational structure, and its culture. Commonly, the committee will minimally include the IT executive sponsor and a representative from the business side of the house to handle day-to-day tasks. For larger initiatives, the steering committee may well include other business stakeholders along with a dedicated staff to actively oversee the initiative.

Ideally, the business executive sponsor is also the chairperson of the steering committee. When major decisions are required, the business executive sponsor is there to call the shots. If time does not permit this direct participation, the steering committee itself provides the day-to-day oversight of the projects under the initiative, reporting progress to the business sponsor. *However, in such cases, the responsibilities delegated to the steering committee should not extend to making changes to the overall project goals, budget, and schedule, nor should they include the authority to make major decisions related to project and business process risk.* These decisions must remain the responsibility of the business executive sponsor, for their impact will extend well beyond the boundaries of this initiative.

The Enterprise Projects Organization

While large initiatives may warrant the establishment of steering committees, what are you to do with the growing number of smaller projects? Who will provide their day-to-day oversight since the business executive sponsor obviously will not have time? The reality is that in most organizations, this question remains unanswered. The result is that there is no effective communication between the project team and the business executive sponsor. This makes it nearly impossible to raise the visibility of priority misalignments. The consequence is that misalignments go unresolved unless the project manager raises enough of a stink to get the attention of the business executive sponsor. Since such exercises often shorten careers, this tactic is rarely used. Issues remain unresolved, and the project's true business objectives are not realized.

The solution to this problem is to create an enterprise projects organization to which all enterprise-scale projects—projects that span silos—report (Figure 6–6). This organization, in turn, reports to the business executive sponsor. Essentially, this enterprise projects organization plays the same role as a major initiative steering committee.

You must recognize that while the enterprise projects organization may provide the day-to-day oversight needed for enterprise projects, only the business executive sponsor has the real authority to compel cooperation among all participants. As such, the enterprise projects organization must provide an open and effective communications channel between each project manager and the business executive sponsor. The project manager and the enterprise projects organization will most often try to persuade silo managers to cooperate, but unsuccessful attempts at securing cooperation indicate the presence of conflicts

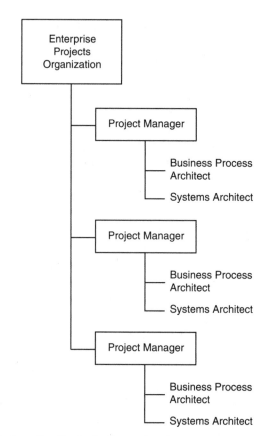

Figure 6–6: *Enterprise Projects Organization*

between the project's priorities and those of the silo owners. Only the executive sponsor can resolve these conflicts, and delays in obtaining their resolution will only cause delays and inefficiencies in the projects. Thus an open and frank project status dialog with the executive sponsor is essential for project success.

Oversight Team Responsibilities

Whether the project is being overseen by the business executive sponsor directly, a major initiative steering committee, or an enterprise projects organization, the oversight team has four major responsibilities with respect to each project:

1. Chartering the project
2. Establishing project feasibility

amazon.com

Billing Address:
Ruth Allison
2655 E King Rd
Kuna, ID 83634-2409
United States

Shipping Address:
Ruth Allison
2655 E King Rd
Kuna, ID 83634-2409
United States

Returns Are Easy!
Visit http://www.amazon.com/returns to return any item -including gifts- in unopened or original
condition within 30 days for a full refund (other restrictions apply)

Your order of June 15, 2008 (Order ID: 105 — 8181447 — 0020231)

Qt.	Item	Item Price	Total
	IN THIS SHIPMENT		
1	**Succeeding with SOA: Realizing Business Value Through Total A...** 0321508912 0321508912 0321508912 Paperback	$29.25	$29.25

SubTotal	$29.25
Shipping & Handling	$3.99
Promotional Certificate	-$3.99
Order Total	$29.25
Paid via Amex	$29.25
Balance due	$0.00

This shipment completes your order.

(1 of 1)

amazon.com
and you're done.™

182/Dxw095nVR/ 1 of 1-//1M/econ-us/3955188/0620-00 30/0618-00 06 BA8

3. Fostering cooperation
4. Measuring success

Chartering the Project

The first responsibility of the oversight team is to charter the project. The project charter establishes the goals of the project, identifies the key personnel on both the oversight and project teams, and establishes the governance process that will be used to oversee the project.

From the business perspective, perhaps the most challenging aspect of chartering the project lies in quantifying its business goals. Because quantifying the expected benefits provides a measurable definition of success, it provides a clear focus for the project team. Since the project team will be held accountable for achieving these goals, the project charter should also specify how this success will be measured and require that those measurements be made once the system has been placed into production.

The oversight team should take care to ensure that these measurements accurately reflect the true intent of the project. These measurements will become the driving force behind the project and may well become the basis for incentives for the project leadership team. The charter must also quantify project constraints (cost and schedule guidelines) and business consequences arising from over- and underachieving the project goals.

The project charter must also identify who will play each of the five key leadership roles for the project: the business executive sponsor, the IT executive sponsor, the project manager, the business process architect, and the systems architect. The project charter must clearly indicate the reporting structure of the project team. If the project manager does not report directly to the business executive sponsor, the charter must clearly lay out the roles and responsibilities of the oversight team members and the corresponding reporting structure.

The final task in chartering the project is to provide the budgetary and personnel resources necessary to conduct the project. The business and IT executive sponsors must establish that their respective resources are actually available, although they may not all be committed at once. The initial commitment is to provide sufficient resources to reach a conclusion regarding the project feasibility. Then, if the outcome is favorable, the business executive sponsor can commit the remaining resources needed to complete the work.

Establishing Project Feasibility

Perhaps the most important responsibility of the oversight team is to verify that the project is feasible within the given cost and schedule guidelines. You have to recognize that the guidelines initially given to the project are not estimates. They are a statement of the level of investment that the enterprise is willing to make in order to achieve the specified benefits. There may well be a gap between this anticipated level of investment and that actually required to reach the goals. This gap represents a risk, and the oversight team is responsible for managing risk.

Because of this potential gap between the project's cost and schedule guidelines and the actual effort it will take, it is prudent for the oversight team to direct the project team to explicitly determine the feasibility of providing the expected benefits within these guidelines. The oversight team should direct the project team to structure its work so as to provide this feasibility feedback early in the project and to do so with minimal time and resource investment. (I will discuss how to go about doing this in Chapter 9.) Should the feedback indicate that there is a gap, obtaining this information early affords maximum flexibility in the use of the remaining time and resources.

Besides obtaining early feasibility feedback, there is another distinct advantage to this approach. The project leadership team is being given an explicit choice as to whether or not to accept the project on the terms outlined in the project charter. Should the team members determine that the project is feasible, they will be making a well-considered commitment to deliver the expected benefits within the cost and schedule guidelines. This level of personal commitment is a powerful self-motivator and can be obtained only by offering the choice.

Of course, the oversight team must also be prepared to accept feedback that these ends are not achievable, at least not within the project's initial guidelines. The oversight team must take care not to discourage the reporting of such bad news. Doing so will only result in more time and resources being spent before the bad news finally surfaces—but it will always surface! The problem is that it may not happen until user acceptance testing or after deployment, by which time virtually all of the time and resources will have been expended. The only options left will be to spend whatever additional time and money are required or to kill the project. Encouraging early feedback preserves the option to redirect these resources in a more productive direction.

In the event that the project team determines that the project is not feasible, the oversight team needs to work with the project team to find a cost/benefit mix that makes sense for the business. The project methodology outlined in Chapter 9 will provide the project team with ample information about alternatives worth considering and the projected costs to complete.

Fostering Cooperation

Another major responsibility of the oversight team is to ensure the active cooperation of all participants vital to the project. As the project progresses and the scope of the involved systems and organizations unfolds, the oversight team must reach out to the managers of the groups involved and ensure that their personnel become active members of the project team. Passive resistance on the part of business operational teams and system owners has killed more than its share of projects over the years.

As discussed earlier, a common mechanism for ensuring cooperation is incentive compensation. The oversight team, and the business executive sponsor in particular, must ensure that silo incentives are aligned with project goals. Nonaligned incentives will, at a minimum, create conflicts for participants. Worst case, they will lead silo managers to passively or actively resist the changes being made by the project team. Such resistance will result in costly delays or the outright failure of the project.

Incentives are the carrot part of the cooperation equation, but the oversight team and business executive sponsor must be prepared to employ the stick as well. When the project team is unable to obtain the needed cooperation voluntarily, this failure must be communicated to the oversight team. The oversight team must then take action to attain the needed cooperation. This is another point at which the full span of authority of the business executive sponsor may be required.

Measuring Success

The final responsibility of the oversight team is to determine whether or not the project has succeeded—whether the expected benefits have been realized. This determination requires measuring the level of benefit achieved once the processes and systems have been deployed. Since these measurements might not be a natural by-product of the business processes, it is important that the measurement criteria be established when the project is chartered and that the collection of this measurement data be made a project requirement. Until these benefit measurements have been collected and evaluated, the real success or failure of the project remains indeterminate.

The oversight team must also determine how much of the project team should be left in place in this initial operational period while success is being measured. These project team members will be needed to make any additional changes required to achieve the desired benefits fully. Deciding how many people to leave on the project is a risk/reward tradeoff. Removing people too soon will certainly reduce the short-term project cost, but it will increase the time and effort required to make subsequent changes. When changes are required, the needed resources must first be located and brought into the project. On the other hand, keeping too many people on the project will increase the project cost, though it will shorten the response time for making changes.

During this transitional period, the oversight team must provide feedback to the project team as to whether, in its opinion, the expected benefits are being satisfactorily achieved. If they are not, the two teams must work together to define a remediation plan. Ideally, any required changes will be achievable within the project's original cost and schedule guidelines. If not, the oversight team must make a judgment as to whether the charter should be updated to reflect the increase in cost and schedule or the project should be terminated. Following the methodology outlined in Chapter 9 and detailed in the companion volume, *SOA in Practice: Implementing Total Architecture*, will minimize the likelihood of such outcomes.

Political Realities

In an ideal situation, the entire project team would be fully aware of all of the business drivers (benefits, constraints, risks, and so on) behind the project. All of this information would be contained in the project charter, which I will detail in Chapter 11. The charter will then provide a shared vision and focus for the entire project team. However, under some conditions, portions of this information may be sensitive, particularly when competitive positioning, downsizing, or remediation for regulatory or contractual noncompliance is involved. In these cases, the oversight team must decide how much of this information will be contained in the published project charter.

However, regardless of how much information is actually placed in the written charter, it is essential that the full project circumstances be shared with the project team leadership. Whether those circumstances are communicated verbally or otherwise, the project manager, business process architect, and systems architect all need to understand the actual situation in order to guide the project team appropriately.

In the absence of such understanding, they may end up making decisions that are inconsistent with the true objectives for the project. The inadequacy of these decisions will not become evident until very late in the project, and the consequences may range from simple cost overruns to outright project failure. Remember, for mission-critical projects, project failure may also equate to enterprise failure. The project team leadership needs to know what is at stake in order to direct the project appropriately.

Oversight Team Summary

To ensure project success, the oversight team must carry out the four broad responsibilities outlined earlier: chartering the project, determining project feasibility, ensuring the cooperation of participants, and measuring actual results. There are many ways to organize this oversight team, but regardless of its organization, the role of the business executive sponsor remains critical. All decisions and all risks are ultimately this person's responsibility. Regardless of the oversight team's constitution, the business executive sponsor should make all of the major decisions. The second most important role is that of the IT executive sponsor, and the charter should make clear the reporting relationship between this person and the business executive sponsor. Whatever the actual organization of the balance of the oversight team, the project charter must clearly define its makeup and organization, as it constitutes the governance body for the project team.

Organizational Variations for Project Oversight

The organizational structures depicted in this chapter represent ideals. I do not mean to imply that projects and enterprises have to be organized in exactly this manner in order to succeed. What I will say is that projects and enterprises that do succeed have found an effective means of addressing each of the issues discussed in this chapter. In particular, they have consistently found a way to align silo priorities and get the right people to focus their energies on delivering real business value.

Project Teams Report to IT

The most common variation you are likely to encounter is that the project teams report into the IT side of the house and not the business side. This, in fact, is the more traditional home for these projects. This approach works as long as the business units are tolerant of the project team poking into the whys and wherefores of the business process and are willing to cooperate with the project team in developing improved business processes as well as improved information systems. The project team will reach an impasse, however, the minute such cooperation ends. Short of raising the visibility of the issue up through the CIO to the COO or CEO, there is little the project team can do to evolve business processes and ensure that the project delivers business value. How will such problems be resolved in your organization?

Another issue you are likely to encounter with projects reporting into the IT side of the house is that the IT community may resist business requirements that require significant IT investments. A common example arises in the discussion of business continuity requirements. It may be a business requirement that a specific business process must continue operating at a specific location even when communication to the central data center is lost. Hotel guests, for example, must be able to check in regardless of the hotel's ability to communicate with any remote data center.

Satisfying this business continuity requirement may require specific information (or some more complete set of functionality) to be physically present at that location. This may sound simple from a business perspective, but the IT community is well aware of the cost and complexity implications. If that location is not a data center, this may require the establishment of a new technology footprint at the location to house the information or perform the function. This, in turn, will require provisions for operating and maintaining that equipment along with additional infrastructure to back up and restore information. These are nontrivial investments.

In this example, both sides have legitimate concerns, but ultimately someone has to make a judgment call as to whether the business requirement warrants the investment. Who will make this call in your organization? More importantly, who has the authority to compel compliance with the decision—an authority that extends to allocating budget as well as personnel resources?

The Split Team

A less common and more complex variation is to have a pair of project teams, one on the business side of the house and the other on the technical side. This solves the problem of business cooperation but ignores the tight connectivity between the business process design and systems design. To make this approach work, close cooperation and coordination between the two project teams is required, particularly between the business process architect and the systems architect. Close cooperation is also needed between the two oversight teams. Disagreements and misalignment of priorities at the oversight level will misalign the objectives of the two project teams and jeopardize the success of the overall project. The business continuity example would pose a major challenge to a split-team approach.

Summary

SOA projects and other enterprise-scale initiatives span the traditional organizational boundaries separating business units. As such, they pose several organizational challenges. One challenge lies in determining what each organizational unit (silo) needs to do in order to achieve the project's overall business goals. Silo-oriented development processes lack the explicit architectural step required to make this determination. If your organization lacks this step in its development process, you must reintroduce this activity along with an explicit project charter to establish the common project goal and an integration test step to manage the initial integration.

However, figuring out what different organizations need to do solves only part of the problem. Each organization must be willing to play its part. A problem arises when organizational priorities do not align with the business priorities motivating the project. Such misalignments lead to organizational resistance and project failure. To make your SOA projects effective, you must ensure that organizational priorities are aligned through the efforts of business and IT executive sponsors.

Ideally, project teams report to the business side of the house, where project budgets originate and project benefits accrue. This reporting structure directly addresses the priority alignment issue. However, many businesses choose to have projects report into the IT side of the house, or they decide to split the project team into a business team reporting to the business side and an IT ream reporting to the IT side. These alternatives create situations in which it is difficult to make balanced tradeoffs between business requirements and IT costs and to enforce the resulting decisions. If you employ these approaches in your organization, you must determine how such tradeoffs will be made and decisions enforced.

In the real world, it is unlikely that any enterprise you encounter will ever provide an exact match to the organizational ideals presented in this chapter. What you need to do is examine your organizational structures and understand the extent to which they are successfully addressing the questions raised in this chapter. Where issues are not being successfully addressed, you must ask what organizational changes you need to make. Where changes are needed, you will most likely need to define a transition plan to evolve from the current organizational structure to the revised structure without disrupting existing business processes and ongoing development projects.

Key Organizational Questions

1. Who is responsible for silo-spanning projects? Are they responsible for the business process design as well as the systems design? Do they report to the business side of the house? If not, who provides the balance between business and IT needs?

2. Who oversees and governs silo-spanning projects? Who ensures the cooperation of individual business and IT silos for silo-spanning projects? How are differences in business and IT priorities resolved?

3. Does the design methodology used for silo-spanning projects include an explicit architecture step? Does the architecture step address both business process architecture and systems architecture? Is there a step for integration testing?

Suggested Reading

Armour, Philip G. 2006. "The Operational Executive Sponsor." *Communications of the ACM*, 49(3): 15–18.

Chapter 7

SOA Project Leadership

The project leadership team actively runs the project. It is comprised of a project manager, a business process architect, and a systems architect. The project manager focuses on resources, budget, and schedule. The business process architect focuses on the changes to the business process that will be required to deliver the expected benefits. The systems architect determines the systems changes that will be required and oversees the implementation of these changes. Together, the project leadership team is responsible for delivering the expected project benefits to the enterprise.

As with the oversight team, there are many ways that the project team might be organized. All of these variations, however, depend on these three critical project leadership roles: the project manager, the business process architect, and the systems architect. *These are likely to be the only people in a position to see the connection between the project work and the business benefit it is supposed to generate.*

The Project Manager

The project manager is responsible for the overall project from its very inception through its conclusion. Traditionally, the project manager has focused narrowly on managing the development team's activities as it makes systems changes. While this remains an important responsibility, such a scope is too narrow to ensure the success of multisilo projects. Tight interdependencies between business processes and their supporting systems require that the business process and systems changes be made concurrently. Thus the project must include the business process design activities as well as the systems development activities. Ultimately, *the **project manager** is responsible for ensuring that the combined business process and systems changes actually generate the project's expected business benefits within the cost and schedule guidelines.* The project manager is responsible for organizing both business and systems resources from the start of the project initialization through the realization of the expected benefits.

To achieve these ends, the project manager must collaborate closely with the business process and systems architects. Together, these three ensure that the project produces practical business processes and systems capable of delivering the expected business benefits. Furthermore, they ensure that the needed changes can be implemented within the project's cost and schedule guidelines. This scope of responsibility encompasses all modifications to both the business processes and systems and continues until measurable business benefits have been demonstrated.

Bringing business process development into the mix means that the project manager must oversee the participation of business operations personnel as well as development personnel. Business operations personnel are the people who actually execute the business processes and operate the systems on a daily basis. Their involvement is critical, as they are the ones who must ultimately commit to delivering the expected business benefits. The need to ensure that the revised business processes and systems fit smoothly into their world makes their participation in the project essential.

You can expect that the scope of operations personnel involved in the project will likely expand during the course of the project. This will occur as the architects identify additional related business processes and systems that are the sources of required inputs or the destinations of results. If these additional processes and systems need to be modified, the relevant operations personnel must be brought into the project team.

One of the project manager's main responsibilities is resource planning and project scheduling. Since the majority of the project's resources will likely come from the business silos, this involves a lot of negotiation with the silos. This is one area (but not the only one) in which the participation of the business and IT executive sponsors is essential to align the silo priorities with the charter of the project.

Another major responsibility of the project manager is to provide air cover for the business process and systems architects. The business process and system changes needed to achieve the overall business benefit may run counter to the interests and concerns of the individual silos. This is often the result of a misalignment between silo priorities and project needs. The project manager assists the business process and systems architects in obtaining the cooperation of the silos. If these efforts are unsuccessful, the project manager must then seek the assistance of the oversight team, specifically the business and IT executive sponsors. The sponsors are the only people with the authority to resolve the situation.

The Business Process Architect

The business process architect is responsible for defining the overall business process and, more specifically, for identifying the business process changes that will be required to produce the expected business benefits. I use the term *business process architect* rather than the more traditional *business analyst* in order to emphasize that this role involves much more than analysis. *The **business process architect** determines the structure and organization of the overall business process.* Since structure and organization are the very definition of architecture, I use the term *architect* for this role. In architecting the business processes, the architect will determine which business silos will perform which activities and when. The architect will determine which activities will be performed by people and which by systems. He or she will determine how the business process will respond to errors and exceptions and what kind of business process monitoring will be required to effectively manage the process.

It is absolutely essential to recognize that this role of business process architect does not yet exist in most enterprises. In fact, in most enterprises, there isn't anyone who knows what the current business processes look like. (Try to find someone who can tell you how a new employee is brought on board, and don't accept generalities for answers. You will find people who know fragments of the process in great detail, but it is unlikely that you will find anyone with the complete picture.) It is likely that even the individual organizational responsibilities in this process and the handoffs between them are ill defined and poorly understood.

All too often, the only people who can truly see the overall business process are your customers and business partners. This can be painfully obvious to a customer who is trying to rectify a mistake made by your business processes. The business process may make it easy for a customer to reserve and pay for an airline seat in a matter of minutes, but just try to cancel the reservation and obtain a refund! It may be days or weeks before the money is back in the customer's hands. Even more challenging is to try to obtain a status report on that refund. Such situations illustrate how poorly we really understand end-to-end enterprise business processes.

How, then, can you hope to monitor, manage, and improve something you don't understand? As described in Chapter 2, making changes to business processes without understanding how they work is a dicey proposition at best. You badly need this business process architect role in your projects and in your business.

The business process architect must work hand in hand with the systems architect to ensure that it is practical for systems to play their expected roles. This is best accomplished by having the systems architect directly participate in the business process definition. Both architects must then work with the project manager to determine whether the combined business process and systems changes can be implemented within the project's cost and schedule guidelines.

The Systems Architect

*The **systems architect** determines the structure and organization of the information systems supporting the business processes.* The basic responsibility is to ensure that the resulting architecture effectively supports the business processes as defined by the business process architect. In so doing, the systems architect defines the needed components and services as well as the interplay between them that will be required to support the business processes. This person then specifies those individual components and services and oversees their implementation and testing. The systems architect works with the project manager to determine whether these systems changes can be implemented within the project's cost and schedule guidelines.

Since most of the needed systems resources and development resources reside in silos that are not under the direct control of the project, the systems architect must work closely with the IT organizations in the various business process silos to hammer out the overall systems architecture. This architecture not only will specify the roles and responsibilities of the system components but also, by implication, will determine which IT organizations will be responsible for developing, maintaining, and operating each of the components and services.

Which IT organization should be responsible for developing which component may seem obvious—at least until new technologies are introduced. It is not uncommon for an enterprise to create a new IT organization to manage the introduction of new technology. This is particularly the case for technologies related to messaging, application integration, services, and business process management. These technologies are used to gain access to or manage functionality in existing systems.

The result of introducing integration and services technologies is that providing functionality now requires a collaboration between the new technology and the existing systems—and between the new organization and the existing silo. In such cases, the systems architect must determine which responsibilities are appropriate for this new organization and which responsibilities should remain with the business silo. This is especially true for services, where the new technology typically provides the interface and systems in the existing silo provide the actual functionality. Something as simple as a service-level agreement (SLA) for the service's response time involves commitments from both organizations. Technical decisions require organizational commitments.

Project Leadership Team Responsibilities

The project leadership team's responsibilities are summed up in the project prime objective: to determine whether the expected benefits are attainable within the cost and schedule guidelines; if they are, deliver the benefits within the guidelines. Realizing the expected business benefits involves more than just making the changes to the business processes and systems. The benefits are realized during the operation of the updated business processes and systems.

Consequently, if you want to know whether the changes you have made are producing the expected benefits, you have to operate the business processes and systems and then measure the results. This measurement and the guidance of remedial activity are also part of the project leadership team's responsibilities. These responsibilities continue until the oversight team concludes either that the expected benefits are being realized or that further efforts toward achieving them are no longer warranted.

The project prime objective breaks down into four major responsibilities for the project leadership team.

1. Define the solution that will produce the expected benefits.
2. Determine whether the project is feasible—whether the solution can be delivered within the project's cost and schedule guidelines. If the project is feasible, commit to producing the benefits.
3. Make the changes to the enterprise's business processes and systems, and deploy the changes into production.
4. Deliver the benefits. Determine whether the updated business processes and systems are actually delivering the expected benefits, and take appropriate action.

Defining the Solution

The solution is comprised of the revised business processes and systems required to produce the expected benefits. The project responsibility is not just to define the *changes* that will be required. It is to define the *completed business processes and systems* and to determine whether those modified processes and systems, when placed into service, will produce the desired business benefits. I emphasize the need to define the full business processes and systems because otherwise the thorough understanding of the current business process and systems architecture often becomes lost as successive projects document only the changes they make. This makes it difficult to understand the true consequences of proposed changes in future projects, and it greatly complicates the monitoring and troubleshooting of business processes and systems.

While there is a natural tendency for a project to focus on those business processes and systems that are directly involved in producing the desired benefits, the solution may also involve other business processes and systems. These related business processes and systems produce inputs required by the primary business processes or consume their results. The project leadership team needs to determine whether these related processes need to be changed in any way. If so, these changes must be included within the scope of the project as they can significantly impact the project's cost and schedule. Unless you make a conscious effort to identify these secondary changes, it is easy to overlook them early in the project lifecycle. The result is that their cost and schedule impact comes as an unpleasant surprise later in the project. This is an unnecessary and avoidable risk.

While the business process and systems architects have the responsibility for defining the overall solution, the operations personnel from the various silos play a critical role as well. These people not only provide input to the solution definition but also must concur that these changes are capable of delivering the expected benefits. In fact, these are the people who will actually employ the revised business processes and systems to actually deliver the benefits. The project leadership team cannot commit to delivering the benefits without their concurrence.

Determining Project Feasibility

Having a solution that generates the expected benefits does not, by itself, meet the project prime objective. That objective requires making the changes within the project's cost and schedule guidelines. Thus, establishing project feasibility requires determining whether or not the benefits are achievable within those guidelines.

Stating that the project is feasible actually represents commitments from both development and operations personnel. The development personnel, led by the business process and systems architects, must commit to designing and implementing the required business process and system changes within the cost and schedule guidelines. The operations personnel must commit to using the updated business processes and systems to produce the expected benefits, again within cost and schedule guidelines. This is an acknowledgment that project constraints may include expectations concerning operational efficiency and expenses, and these expectations must be included within this operational commitment.

While the project manager is responsible for determining feasibility and obtaining these commitments, you must recognize that the operational commitment is coming from the business silos. Because of this, a significant portion of the project manager's responsibility is to socialize the proposed solution with the various business silos in order to obtain this operational commitment. The assistance of the business process and systems architects is essential in this endeavor, as the architects are the only people who can articulate the overall solution and the manner in which it will produce the benefits.

There is, of course, another possible outcome at this stage. The project leadership team might conclude that the benefits cannot actually be achieved within the given cost and schedule constraints. In this case, the project leadership team must articulate to the oversight team exactly why this is so. In this conversation, the project leadership team should provide an accurate cost and schedule estimate for achieving the benefits as specified but may also propose modified sets of goals and constraints for the oversight team's consideration. You must keep in mind, however, that at the end of the day, it is the business executive sponsor who must make any decision altering the charter of the project.

Making the Changes

Once the project has been deemed feasible, the project leadership team has the responsibility of making the business process and system changes required to produce the expected benefits. This, of course, must be accomplished within the now-committed cost and schedule guidelines. This phase of the project is typically led by the project manager and is focused largely on the development activity. However, keep in mind that issues will arise, and refinements to the solution are inevitable. The business process and systems architects must remain involved to resolve any issues. Addressing these issues may require solution changes that alter the operational aspects of the business process. In such cases, the operations personnel need to be involved once again in reviewing these changes to ensure that they are consistent with the operational concept and do not adversely impact the utility of the solution.

The actual work of implementing the systems changes is typically carried out by personnel belonging to the individual organizational silos. The detailed responsibilities of the project leadership team with respect to this development work will vary depending on how your organization chooses to organize this work.

One way of organizing the development work is to have the developers report (dotted-line) to the project leadership team. This requires the leadership team to take on the development management role as well. The team members will oversee the management of the changes to each component or service, possibly requiring additional staff to manage this activity. With this type of project organization, the project leadership team must negotiate with each silo to obtain the resources it needs. The leadership team then runs the project as a single virtual team.

Alternatively, each silo retains the responsibility for managing its own development work. Each silo has its own development manager overseeing the evolution of that silo's components and services. The project leadership team negotiates with each development manager to establish the requirements (i.e., the component and service specifications), budget (time and material), and schedule for that silo's work. With this type of project organization, the processes for individual silo status tracking and component technical review must be established. The project leadership team must also determine who will be responsible for staff integration testing and overall system testing as well.

Once development and testing are complete, the actual deployment of the changes marks a major milestone in the project. It marks the formal handoff from development personnel to operations personnel. Prior to this milestone, the development personnel have been leading the effort with the support of the operations personnel. After this milestone, the operations personnel take the lead with the support of the development personnel.

Delivering the Benefits

Once the changes have been deployed, the operations personnel are now using the updated business processes and systems with the expectation that they will deliver the expected benefits. You must recognize, however, that initially the ability of these changes to produce the benefits is just a conjecture. Thus, the project team must collect data for some period of time after deployment to measure the extent of the benefit actually being realized. These measurements must then be shared with the oversight team, who will make the final determination as to whether the expected benefits have been sufficiently realized. During this measurement period, the development team may need to make further alterations to the business processes and systems. The responsibilities of the project leadership team do not end until the oversight team is satisfied with the results—or concludes that further efforts are not warranted.

Organizational Variations for Project Leadership

The three project leadership roles presented in this chapter represent an ideal for running a project. This does not mean that projects must be organized this way in order to be successful. However, successful projects will manage, somehow, to cover the responsibilities of the project manager, business process architect, and systems architect as laid out in this chapter.

The IT-Centric Project

One common deviation from the ideal scenario occurs when the project reports to the IT side of the house rather than the business side. When this happens, the project leadership team is typically not responsible for delivering the business value and designing the business process. Unfortunately, this does not obviate the need to do either.

Under such circumstances, a successful project leadership team will still address these issues even though it is not officially responsible for them. This is accomplished through simply asking questions of the business side of the house. Through these questions, the project leadership team begins to assemble a picture of the expected business value and the business process expected to deliver this value. The goal is to determine whether the business process has been thought through and whether the business process appears reasonably capable of delivering the expected benefits.

The technique is to use carefully posed questions that draw attention to portions of the business process or business goals that do not seem to be well defined. The weakness of this approach, of course, is that the project leadership team is completely dependent on the willingness of the business side of the house to participate in this exercise. The project leadership team is not really in a position to drive the business process definition and keep its modification focused on achieving the business goals. They also need the support of the project oversight team to expend resources on the business side of the problem.

A variation on this theme is the total absence of the business process architect. In other words, nobody is charged with the explicit responsibility for designing the business processes. Under these circumstances, the systems architect often ends up playing this role by taking the initiative and modeling the business processes as a first step toward implementing the systems support for these processes. Once again, the technique of carefully posed questions can be used to uncover the business process definitions and draw attention to portions of the process that are not fully defined. To be successful in this endeavor, the systems architect will require the support of the project manager and oversight team, along with the cooperation of the business side of the house.

The Virtual Leadership Team

A different kind of variation you may encounter is that the project leadership team itself comprises a virtual team. The business process and systems architects come from their respective organizations and have dotted-line reporting responsibilities to the project manager. The chief risk here is one of conflicting time commitments. The business process and systems architects may have other competing demands for their time. To the extent that they are distracted from the needs of the project, the project as a whole will suffer.

This problem can be very serious if it turns out to be a symptom of conflicting priorities, an issue that we discussed in the previous chapter. If IT priorities are different from business priorities, the systems architect and business process architect may be drawn in very different directions and have very different views of what the project objectives are. Since the project relies on these two individuals to drive business processes and systems toward achieving these objectives, such priority conflicts will cause the project to fail. You must ensure that such conflicts do not arise, or your SOA efforts will be for naught.

Summary

The project leadership team focuses the project on achieving its chartered goals. This team is comprised of three roles: the project manager, business process architect, and systems architect. The project manager has overall responsibility for achieving the project objectives, which are to realize the business benefits expected from the project. The business process architect is responsible for determining the business process changes that will be required to achieve these benefits, and the systems architect is responsible for determining the systems changes required to support the revised business processes. Together, these three people are responsible for determining whether the expected benefits can be achieved within the cost and schedule guidelines.

Determining the feasibility of achieving the expected benefits within the given guidelines is the principal order of business for the leadership team when the project begins. This work requires determining what each of the silo organizations needs to do in order to achieve these goals—both development work and operational business process work. The leadership team must work with the individual silos to determine what needs to be done and negotiate agreements to get it done.

Regardless of whether or not the project leadership team has official responsibility for the business processes and business results, if its members do not pay attention to the total architecture, nobody else will. The successful project leadership team will take on these responsibilities regardless of their formal responsibilities. This becomes critical when systems are deeply embedded in the business processes and multiple organizational silos are involved.

Key Project Leadership Questions

1. Are your project managers responsible for delivering the expected business benefits from a project? If not, who is?
2. Who is responsible for determining what business process changes will be required to deliver the expected business benefits?
3. Who designs the overall business process and determines the roles that different business units and systems will play in that process?
4. Who is responsible for the end-to-end systems design and ensuring that it supports the business process?
5. Who is responsible for determining whether the planned solution can be implemented within the project's cost and schedule guidelines?
6. Who commits to delivering the expected business benefits?

Chapter 8

SOA Enterprise Leadership

Most of the discussion up to this point has focused narrowly on the work of a single project and the business processes and systems impacted by that project. However, many of the architectural issues you encounter in projects extend well beyond the boundaries of a single project, just as the enterprise projects you have been considering span multiple business silos. The lifetimes of business processes, applications, business services, databases, and supporting infrastructure extend well beyond the boundaries of any given project. Consequently, any alterations to these architectural elements require a perspective beyond that of a single project. This is the role of the enterprise architecture group: to provide that perspective and oversee any architectural changes whose impacts extend beyond the boundaries of an individual project.

The Elements of Enterprise Architecture

The elements of the enterprise architecture, from the network infrastructure all the way up to the business processes themselves, are incredibly interdependent (Figure 8–1). You can hardly touch one without impacting another. Despite this, companies often organize

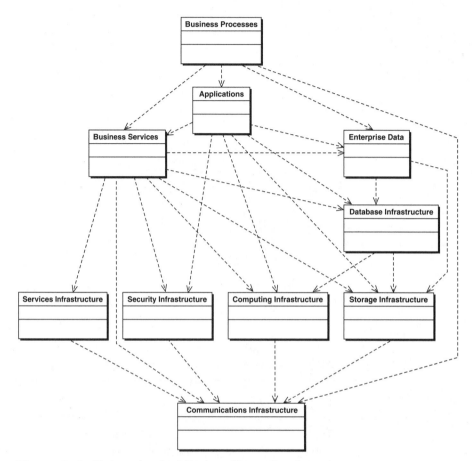

Figure 8–1: *Enterprise Architecture Dependencies*

themselves as if each type of architectural element were independent of the others. In the past, they have created network groups, database groups, computing resources groups, and application development groups. Now they find themselves asking whether they ought to be creating a SOA services group as well. The problem with this approach is that these groups are not, in reality, independent.

Until now, companies have gotten away with fragmenting enterprise responsibilities. Individual architectural groups have gotten together, as needed, to work out the interdependencies between their respective areas. This approach works reasonably well for silo-centric development, when decisions made within one silo have little impact on other silos. However, increasing business pressures are now shifting the enterprise focus toward improving end-to-end business processes involving multiple silos. This brings systems integration and service-oriented architecture to the forefront, and suddenly these interdependencies between architectural elements become a dominant concern. Business processes and business services, in particular, are so dependent on other aspects of the architecture that you can scarcely touch these architectural elements without impacting business processes and services. Business services themselves constitute the building blocks of the business processes. The management of these architectural dependencies becomes an issue unto itself.

These same business pressures are also demanding an increased agility in making changes to business processes and systems. Responding to these pressures requires not only simultaneous changes in multiple business silos but also coordinated changes in many areas of enterprise architecture. Just as you need a cross-silo project leadership team to orchestrate changes to business processes, you also need an enterprise architecture team to coordinate these changes in the architectural infrastructure. The purpose of this enterprise architecture team is two-fold: to ensure that the decisions made in each architectural area are optimal across all areas and to ensure that the collective direction of the enterprise architecture work addresses the needs of the enterprise as a whole.

One subject that brings the issue of dependencies clearly into focus is that of site disaster recovery. The loss of a data center and the resulting switchover to a backup site requires architectural decisions in many different areas: networking, storage, databases, security, and application design, to name but a few. In preparation for a failover, data needs to be replicated across sites. To support this, decisions need to be made as to how this replication will be managed. Replication could be managed by the storage subsystem, the databases, the applications themselves, or some combination of these. This decision will deeply impact the design of applications, services, and business processes.

Further decisions need to be made regarding the management of the failover itself. When a failover occurs, applications, services, and all their supporting infrastructure need to be resurrected at the backup site. Decisions need to be made as to how this will actually be accomplished for networks, storage infrastructure, computing infrastructure, and applications. Details as minor as establishing the identity and network addresses of machines, applications, and services again have a deep impact on application, service, and business process design. All of these decisions need to be tightly coordinated, or the failover simply won't work. Site disaster recovery will, itself, become a disaster.

This naturally raises the question as to who should be responsible for making sure that all of these architectural decisions actually work together to get the job done. You could form a special disaster recovery (business continuity) task force to address these specific issues, but what about all the other enterprise-scale architectural issues? What about the architecture of the business processes, services, and infrastructure that are similarly dependent on coordinated architectural decisions? You need a comprehensive solution that addresses all enterprise-scale architectural issues.

Services pose similar challenges, requiring coordinated decisions in many of these areas. Making services uniformly accessible requires coordinated action in the realms of security, services, computing, and storage infrastructure, all of which depend on the communications infrastructure. Even more complicated is the coordination of services across multiple projects. Service interfaces establish standards within the organization: standards for interacting with operations and for representing information. In practice, business services are developed in a project whose perspective includes only that project's usage of the service. This perspective is not broad enough to define operation interfaces and information representations that will support other usages.

The solution is a proactive and comprehensive enterprise architecture group—a group whose responsibility encompasses business process architecture and data architecture as well as applications, services, and infrastructure (Figure 8–2). This group's architectural responsibility spans the full spectrum from architecture vision through implementation and operation. It spans the selection of technology and the structure and organization of solutions. It spans the structure of business processes and the structure of systems. It spans the total architecture. This group has one singular responsibility: to manage the architecture of the enterprise's business processes, data, and systems to ensure that all the architectural elements fit together and operate in a manner that meets the enterprise's business needs.

The responsibilities of the enterprise architecture group fall into four broad categories:

1. Enterprise architecture definition
2. Enterprise architecture governance

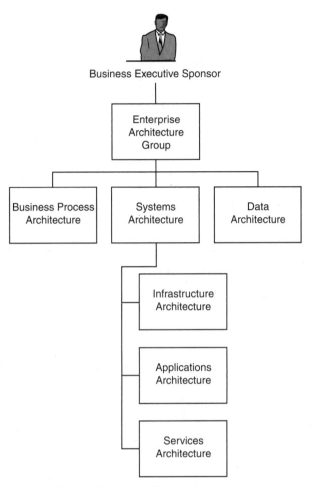

Figure 8–2: *Enterprise Architecture Group*

3. Enterprise architecture standards and best practices
4. Enterprise architecture operation

We will discuss these responsibilities in this chapter.

Enterprise Architecture Definition

By far the most obvious responsibility of the enterprise architecture group is to define the overall enterprise architecture. In contemplating this task, you must recognize that the enterprise architecture is not static—it is constantly changing as business needs vary and technologies evolve. The task of the enterprise architecture group is to guide this evolution. To do so requires that the group keep one eye looking toward the future and the other focused on the realities of the present, while continually striving to draw the two together. Managing this evolution requires understanding the current state, articulating a vision for the future, and defining a roadmap for getting from here to there (Figure 8–3).

The architecture vision paints a picture of the desired architectural state three to five years into the future. It identifies present and anticipated business needs that are not adequately addressed by the present architecture and sketches a future-state architecture that better addresses these needs. These needs can be diverse, from quickly responding to emerging business opportunities through sloughing off the yoke of fragile infrastructure, legacy systems, and antiquated technology.

In order to create the right architecture vision, the enterprise architecture group must understand what is truly important to the enterprise. Whether it is the ability to efficiently handle mergers and acquisitions, improve the customer experience, or cut the cost of operations, the enterprise architecture team requires a clear understanding of business priorities. These priorities will determine the nature of the changes required and, in turn, will guide architectural investments. These priorities must clearly distinguish between the nice-to-have and the must-have capabilities so that the bulk of the investments retain a must-have focus.

The architecture vision must also take into consideration the evolving technology landscape. Emerging technologies must be evaluated to

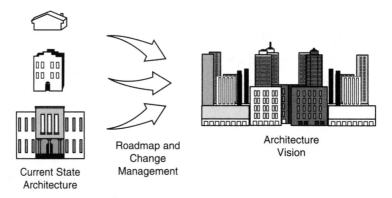

Current State Architecture

Roadmap and Change Management

Architecture Vision

Figure 8–3: *Enterprise Architecture Evolution*

determine the opportunities they might present and to determine the appropriate time to introduce them into the enterprise architecture landscape. An even more challenging task is to lay out a strategy for evolving from the present state to one that embraces the new technologies. An ideal strategy defines a series of incremental changes. Each change produces some real business value while moving incrementally toward the desired end-state architecture. Each incremental change must, however, result in a viable intermediate-state architecture.

Vision and strategy are especially important for your services. A massive replacement of existing interfaces with their service equivalents not only is disruptive but also provides no immediate return on your investment. A viable strategy is key to success. This strategy will likely include an initial investment in services infrastructure coupled with an opportunistic policy for converting functionality to services at such time that the interfaces are being worked on for other reasons. Your strategy must also address adoption of evolving standards as they mature, and it must lay out an interim strategy to bridge the gap.

The architecture vision shows where you are going, but before you can figure out how to get there, you must first determine where you are. Thus, an understanding of the present-state architecture is an essential element of the enterprise architecture. This understanding must encompass business process and systems architecture at both the logical and physical levels. At the logical level, you need to understand today's business processes and how the present architectural components participate in these processes. You need to understand the information that drives these business processes and how that information is managed. Most of all, you need to understand how the various business processes interact with each other to make the enterprise work on a day-to-day basis.

Understanding the present-state architecture also requires knowledge of the physical deployments of the architectural elements in development, test, and production. You need to understand the impact that changes to the physical structure will have on executing business processes. You need to understand what is impacted when you lose a data link, a machine, or a data center. You need to understand how you can detect and respond to breakdowns of both business processes and their supporting systems components. Simply put, you need to understand how the business actually works.

One harsh reality is that such a comprehensive picture of the present-state enterprise architecture most likely does not exist. While you know you need such an understanding to move forward, you have to be pragmatic about how to assemble this picture. You can't just embark on a project to comprehensively capture the present state. Such a project would take years to complete and is liable to produce an understanding that is perpetually out of date.

You need a more pragmatic approach—one that both assembles the required picture and maintains its currency. The way you go about doing this is to focus your immediate attention on projects that are currently in progress or are anticipated to start in the near term. You can focus your energies on understanding those aspects of the present-state architecture that are relevant to these projects. Note that you have to do this anyway in order to have any confidence that the changes you are making will produce the desired results. Keeping in mind that you are really trying to assemble an understanding of the overall enterprise architecture, you require that the project architects document, in a standardized manner, the portion of the architecture they are altering. This documentation must be comprehensive, covering business processes, data, applications, and infrastructure. In this manner, you can build and maintain an increasingly complete picture of the present-state architecture.

You now have a vision of the future and an emerging picture of the present. What remains to be defined is a roadmap detailing how you are going to evolve toward this future state. This roadmap must not only produce the needed changes but also ensure that the enterprise has a viable intermediate-state architecture at every step along the way. Since the enterprise will be in continuous operation during this transition, risk management must be a major consideration while putting this roadmap together. A smooth and rapid progression through a series of small incremental changes will keep each project relatively simple and thus minimize the risks associated with each change.

There is another aspect of this roadmap to consider as well. Businesses expect relatively short-term returns on their investments. Thus, to be effective, the architecture roadmap must lay out a scheme whereby real business value is realized even in the short-term projects while still moving the business toward the future-state architecture. As long as each project provides measurable business value, the investment in the architecture vision can be sustained indefinitely.

This roadmap is an essential element of a viable services strategy. Services, for the most part, are produced in one project but do not provide a return on their investment until their second and subsequent usages.

Generally, these usages occur in subsequent projects. This requires a level of cross-project planning and coordination on two levels: (1) to plan the sequencing of service development and utilization and (2) to ensure that the enterprise begins to realize the return on investment (ROI) you expect from service utilization.

Together, the present-state architecture, architecture vision, and road-map set the stage for a managed enterprise evolution. However, their mere existence does not ensure that the journey will be successful. The vision and roadmap are just sketches, not complete architectural specifications. Furthermore, the present-state picture is incomplete. Thus, as you execute each step of the journey, the present-state understanding will require definition, and the future-state sketches will require interpretation and detail. If you are to arrive at a self-consistent and well-considered future-state architecture, these activities must be performed in a consistent manner from project to project.

The enterprise architecture group is responsible for achieving this consistency across the enterprise. It must manage this architectural modeling and refinement work and interpret the vision and roadmap. Accomplishing this requires a three-pronged attack, involving governance, standards and best practices, and operational support.

Enterprise Architecture Governance

Ensuring that the roadmap and vision are appropriately applied on a project-by-project basis requires architectural governance. Changes to the enterprise architecture, for the most part, occur incrementally. Each project makes small changes as it chooses technologies, alters components, and creates services. The enterprise architecture group must be actively involved with these projects to ensure that these incremental changes all converge into a unified architecture that is consistent with the vision. Enterprise project governance establishes just how and when this involvement occurs.

The enterprise architecture group actually has two responsibilities with respect to project governance: defining the governance process and then participating in it. The specific details of the governance process, deliverables, and governance steps will vary considerably from enterprise to enterprise depending on the culture of the organization and the scale of the project. However, the governance of every project should include, at a minimum, the steps outlined in Table 8–1.

Table 8–1: *Minimum Steps for Project Governance*

Governance Step	Deliverables[a]	Decisions
Project initiation	• Project charter, quantifying expected business benefits along with cost and schedule guidelines.	• Oversight team decision: Is there sufficient business benefit to justify the planned resource expenditure?
Feasibility assessment	• Partial architecture document (described in *SOA in Practice: Implementing Total Architecture*, the companion volume to this book). This document covers the most challenging and complex business processes and the systems required to support them. It shows the required changes and how these changes are expected to achieve the business benefits. • Initial cost estimate based on this architecture.	• Enterprise architecture group decision: Is the proposed architecture sound and consistent with the vision? • Oversight team decisions: Should the project proceed? Does achieving the expected business benefits within the given cost and schedule guidelines appear to be feasible?
Architecture completion	• Completed project architecture document. • Completed component and service architecture documents (as required). • Completed cost estimate.	• Enterprise architecture group decisions: Is the architecture sound and consistent with the enterprise vision? Are services being used and created appropriately? • Oversight team decisions: Should the project proceed? Does achieving the expected benefits still appear feasible within cost and schedule guidelines?

Governance Step	Deliverables[a]	Decisions
One or more traditional design, implementation, and test reviews—specifics driven by the scale of the project and enterprise practices	• Design documents. • Implementation artifacts. • Technical test specifications. • Test results.	• Enterprise architecture group decision: Are the design and implementation consistent with the architecture? • Oversight team decision: Is the project remaining within the cost and schedule guidelines?
Predeployment review	• User acceptance test results • Deployment plan • Risk analysis and mitigation plans	• Oversight team and stakeholder decisions: Is the system ready for production deployment? Has capacity planning been done for existing services that this project will use?
Postdeployment operational review	• Operational measurements of benefits achieved.	• Oversight team decisions: Have business objectives been met? Is further work required?

a. With the exception of the project charter, all deliverables are the responsibility of the project team.

As for the enterprise architecture group's direct participation in the governance process, the heaviest involvement will be in the feasibility assessment and architecture review steps. These governance points are critical, as these are the points at which the project's work can most easily be brought into alignment with the overall enterprise architecture vision with minimal impact on cost and schedule. The utilization of existing services and the creation of new services must be carefully scrutinized at this point.

The importance of conducting a substantive architectural review at these two points cannot be overemphasized. Making architectural changes later in the project will result in additional cost and delays as design, implementation, and test activities are repeated. The prospect of these additional costs and delays creates an impediment to any further architectural modifications. As the project progresses, it becomes increasingly difficult to alter the project's architecture to bring it back into alignment with the enterprise's architecture vision. Eventually, the cost of architectural changes becomes cost-prohibitive. If the project's architecture is not at that point in alignment with the enterprise architecture vision, this places the architecture vision and associated long-range business benefits in jeopardy. For this reason, actually achieving the architecture vision mandates early review and intervention in projects.

In addition to simply participating in governance activities, the enterprise architecture group must also stand ready to be more actively involved in projects that are selecting technologies and developing services. When a project requires decisions whose scope extends beyond the project's boundaries, only the enterprise architecture group can bring the required broad perspective to bear on those choices. One way to accomplish this is to allow these decisions to be made initially by the project team and then subsequently reviewed by the enterprise architecture group at one of the governance steps. However, when technology selection or service development is involved, it is quite likely that the choices made by the project team will require substantial alteration after review. For efficiency, in order to avoid such time-consuming after-the-fact alterations, it is prudent to establish a procedure whereby the project teams can solicit the active participation of the enterprise architecture group as these decisions are being made. To make this work, the enterprise architecture group must respond to these requests in a timely manner, for the project team has deadlines to meet.

Enterprise Architecture Standards and Best Practices

While the project governance process provides several opportunities for the enterprise architecture group to align the project's direction with the overall enterprise vision, making after-the-fact adjustments to project architectures is not a particularly efficient means of achieving this end. Nor is it practical for the enterprise architecture group to become actively involved in every project. Alternatively, progress toward the architecture vision can be facilitated through the development of standards and best practices for the project teams to follow. These comprise a sort of cookbook assembled by the enterprise architecture group to guide project work. For best results, these standards and best practices should encompass the following items.

- *The methodology used to capture requirements and define the business process and systems architecture*: This includes standardizing the human-readable representations of business processes, systems, and data, as well as standardizing the artifacts created by projects. Both methodology and representations are covered extensively in this book's companion volume, which can be used as the basis for such a standard.

- *Architectural design patterns, the common patterns used for solving common problems faced by project teams:* These include design patterns for integrating systems, using the enterprise service bus (ESB), wrapping existing business functionality as business services, and using infrastructure services. Patterns for maintaining business continuity should be established showing acceptable architectural approaches to fault tolerance, high availability, and site disaster recovery. Patterns for monitoring and managing business processes, services, and system components should also be established. It is only through the establishment and enforcement of these patterns that a level of consistency can be established across the enterprise. This consistency is absolutely essential to making business continuity actually work and making business process monitoring practical.

- *Training and mentoring:* Simply providing documentation on methodology and design patterns leaves project teams with the task of wading through the documentation to determine how the methodology and patterns should be applied to the project. This task can be made more efficient if the enterprise architecture group conducts training sessions on these topics. Training is especially important where services are concerned, as building and using services requires a diverse knowledge set that spans supporting services, technologies, and design patterns. This knowledge transfer should be augmented with a mentorship system whereby project architects are assigned mentors from the enterprise architecture group. The mentor is on call to provide guidance and assistance as the project architects gain familiarity with the methodology and design patterns.

Enterprise Architecture Operation

The final responsibility of the enterprise architecture group lies in the realm of operations. It may seem odd at first to charge the enterprise architecture group with the responsibility for providing both the vision for the future and some measure of operational responsibility. However, the reality is that service-oriented architectures and distributed systems can be notoriously difficult to monitor and troubleshoot. The enterprise architects must leverage their end-to-end view of the business processes and supporting systems to ensure that the resulting architecture can be readily monitored and managed.

Monitoring and management begin when the project-level architecture is being formulated. The project-level architect understands the end-to-end business process and the participation of system components in that process in great detail. The next step is to identify the participants in the business process who are best able to report business process status and detect and report business process breakdowns. The final step is to extend the design of those participants to detect and report breakdowns. Similar thinking must be applied to services, particularly with respect to tracking their performance and utilization while they are in operation.

The summary reporting of process status, service status, and breakdown detection is an issue that spans all projects. The enterprise architecture group must architect the mechanisms for handling these reports of status and breakdowns. From real-time business process monitoring through statistical analysis and error handling, the enterprise architecture group must establish the design patterns, common services, and technologies that will be used to address these issues. In the area of error handling, this will require understanding the operational processes and supporting systems that respond to both business process and systems breakdowns.

Beyond simply architecting these monitoring and management mechanisms, however, the members of the enterprise architecture group must stand ready to assist in operational troubleshooting. Their broad perspective puts them in a unique position to evaluate symptoms and guide the troubleshooting process. Thus, it is appropriate for the enterprise architecture group to provide third-tier support for root-cause analysis when business processes and systems fail.

Total Architecture Management

Silo-spanning enterprise projects rely heavily on the enterprise architecture group's broader perspective, particularly when it comes to validating and specifying services and selecting technologies. Because of this reliance, it makes sense to join these two groups into a common organizational structure, as shown in Figure 8–4. This common organization will facilitate these interactions, and it will also support the training and mentoring of project architects, providing a growth path for them into the enterprise architecture group.

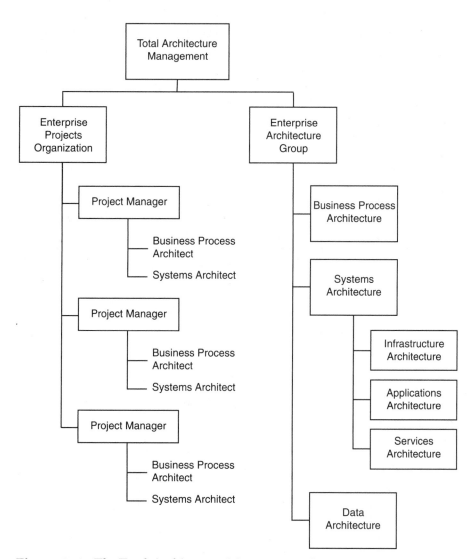

Figure 8–4: *The Total Architecture Management Group*

Stand back now and consider where this total architecture organization might fit into in the overall organizational picture. Since both the enterprise projects group and the enterprise architecture group rely heavily on the support of the business executive sponsor, it would make sense for this combined organization to report to the business executive sponsor. Additionally, the enterprise projects group determines how and when systems integration, services, and business process management technology should be applied. Thus, it would make sense for the IT organization responsible for those technologies (remember the IT organization without a business counterpart shown earlier in Figure 1–4?) to have a dotted-line reporting responsibility to this total architecture management group. We end up with an organization like the one shown in Figure 8–5.

In making this move, you must also consider the relative role of the IT executive sponsor with respect to this new organization. Should the total architecture manager be a peer of the IT executive sponsor? Remember, the total architecture group will be driving the enterprise architecture and making technology selections that impact the IT executive sponsor. In creating the total architecture group, you are effectively refactoring the IT organization, bringing systems architecture and technology selection under the total architecture umbrella and leaving the IT organization as an IT resource management unit.

Alternatively, you might consider folding the IT resource management role into the total architecture organization, merging the role of the IT executive sponsor with the role of total architecture manager. This is tantamount to expanding the role of the IT executive sponsor to encompass business process architecture and thus the realm of the roles and responsibilities of business organizations.

There are pros and cons to combining these roles. On the plus side, combining the roles would certainly guarantee the alignment of IT resource priorities with overall enterprise objectives. On the negative side, the operational aspects of managing all of the IT resources (and none of the business resources) will be time consuming. This resource management activity might consume so much time that the total architecture, that balanced interplay of business processes and systems, would not get the attention it requires.

In reality, the organizational structures presented here are just representative examples of how you might choose to organize your enterprises. You might, for example, build a virtual total architecture organization

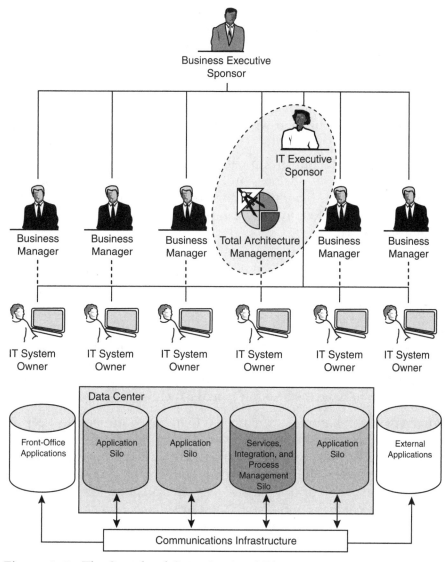

Figure 8–5: *The Completed Organizational Picture*

consisting of a few core members, with the remainder of the members being drawn from other parts of the business and IT organizations and reporting in with dotted-line responsibility. The organizational variations are as numerous as the enterprises themselves.

So how should you apply these concepts to your organizational structures? You simply need to maintain a focus on what is important. This boils down to four points.

1. If you accept the premise of total architecture, that business process and systems architecture are inseparable, then business process and systems architecture must be the assigned responsibility of a single organization with sufficient executive backing to make it work.

2. The total architecture group will, as part of its responsibility, define the architecture of business processes and determine the responsibilities of various operational business units. It is essential for this work to have active executive support on the business side of the house.

3. The total architecture group will, as part of its responsibility, define the services, which effectively define the interfaces of systems belonging to different IT groups. It is essential for this work to have active executive support on the IT side of the house.

4. The most difficult decisions are the judgment calls, and somebody needs to be empowered to call the shots. Consistency in decision making, particularly in converting strategy into execution, is as important as the decisions themselves. Whoever makes these decisions has to have the backing to make them stick.

Whatever organizational structure you choose, you need to keep in mind the importance of establishing strong working relationships between the architectural decision makers and the business and IT executive sponsors. Building the total architecture requires the alignment and balancing of priorities across enterprise projects, enterprise architecture, business units, and IT groups. Executive sponsorship is essential both to achieve the correct balance and to give weight to the architectural decisions. Whatever you do organizationally, you need to be sure that you will achieve the balance between business processes and systems that is required for enterprise success.

Summary

Many different aspects of your business processes and systems require architectural attention, ranging from networks and storage all the way up to applications, services, and the business processes themselves.

While each of these aspects presents its own special challenges, these aspects are also interdependent. Decisions in each area impact decisions in other areas. Furthermore, large-scale initiatives like SOA and site disaster recovery require coordinated decision making across all of these areas.

This situation presents you with the organizational challenge of coordinating the decision making that affects each of these areas as your enterprise architecture evolves. A proactive enterprise architecture group can ensure that these decisions are coordinated and present a coherent whole.

The enterprise architecture group needs to be active in four capacities: enterprise architecture definition, enterprise architecture governance, enterprise architecture standards and best practices, and enterprise architecture operation. This group is responsible for ensuring that the total architecture meets the needs of the business.

The enterprise architecture group and the oversight of enterprise projects need to be considered from an organizational perspective. Both routinely make decisions impacting multiple business and IT groups. You need to carefully consider their organization and organizational positioning, as it will directly impact their effectiveness and hence your total architecture's ability to meet business needs.

Key Organizational Questions

1. Who is responsible for the enterprise architecture? Does that responsibility include the architecture of business processes and business organizational responsibilities? Does it comprehensively encompass all aspects of architecture from business processes right down to the network infrastructure?

2. How are enterprise architecture priorities aligned with business priorities?

3. Who selects new technologies? How are these selections aligned with business priorities, the enterprise architecture, and the needs of individual projects?

4. Who validates business service proposals to ensure that they make sense as services? Who specifies business services to ensure that they will be truly reusable in other contexts? Do they have the broad perspective required to do this effectively?

Chapter 9

Agile SOA Development

So far, I've covered many characteristics of a successful project, such as the need to maintain focus on the business goals and the inseparability of business process and systems design. I've also covered the need for a strong cross-functional team that includes both business process and systems architects, and I've stressed the importance of executive sponsorship. One question remains: How do you actually organize this work?

Just as you want your business processes to provide cost-effective business benefits, you want your project plan to produce the required business processes and its supporting systems in a cost-effective way. You also want an efficient way to determine whether a project is deliverable within its cost and schedule guidelines.

In this chapter, I present a methodology for attacking the design problem called *Total Architecture Synthesis* (TAS), which provides an efficient approach to developing business processes and systems together. When compared with the classic waterfall-style development, this approach significantly reduces project cost, time, and risk. When compared with agile programming, this approach validates architecture suitability before committing to implementation. The methodology leverages the simplicity and precision of standard Unified Modeling Language (UML) design notations to capture the design of both business processes and systems. The use of this common notation for both business process and systems modeling facilitates communication between the business and technical communities and leads to a shared understanding of both business process and system designs.

The Challenge

So what's wrong with the traditional approaches? Suppose you follow a waterfall-style project structure, but in so doing you follow all of the best practices I have discussed so far (Figure 9–1). You charter the project, clearly spelling out the expected business benefit and the cost and schedule guidelines. You embark on a requirements definition phase and a business process synthesis phase that result in well-defined business processes. You then architect the system and move on to specifying the individual components and services. What's wrong with this?

The problem with the waterfall approach is that it does not deal well with complexity. There are many possible designs for business processes and for the systems that support them. Only some of these designs will provide the needed business benefit. Even fewer will provide that benefit within the cost and schedule guidelines. The waterfall approach assumes that each step in the process produces a satisfactory result.

Yet in reality we will not know whether a business process is feasible within the cost and schedule guidelines until we have designed the supporting system. Furthermore, if the project turns out to be infeasible (i.e., there are no designs that satisfy the guidelines, or the specific design you have chosen does not), this may not be discovered until late in the project lifecycle, after you have burned up most of the available time and resources.

TAS is much closer in philosophy to agile development,[1] but here, too, there are differences. Agile development follows the principle that "The most efficient and effective method of conveying information to and within a development team is face-to-face conversation." The reality

---

1. Robert C. Martin, *Agile Software Development, Principles, Patterns, and Practices* (2002), p. 7.

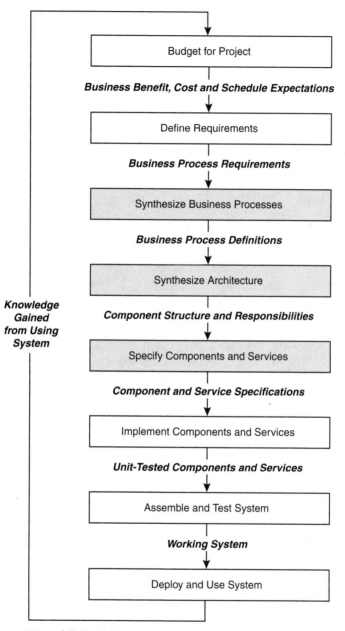

Figure 9–1: *Waterfall-Style Development Highlighting Architectural Activities*

of distributed systems is that they invariably involve multiple development teams, often at multiple locations. As discussed in Chapter 6, the number of organizations involved makes development by face-to-face interaction impractical. Even then, none of the individuals in those organizations has visibility into the end-to-end business processes and systems involved. You need an approach that works for silo-spanning projects that looks beyond the local needs of individual silos.

The basic issue is how to determine whether a project is feasible and to select an appropriate design without burning up all of the time and resources. Two interacting factors make this question difficult to answer: the large number of possible designs and the fact that you can't estimate cost and schedule until a design is at least partially completed. Because of the large number of possible designs, you generally can't afford to explore large numbers of design alternatives, assess the ability of each to provide the expected benefit, and estimate the cost to implement each design. What you need is a way to simplify this search through design alternatives.

The key to simplifying this search lies in an observation: Most requirements are relatively easy to satisfy. Only a small portion of the requirements will present real challenges to the design of your business processes and systems. Furthermore, these difficult requirements will not present a challenge to *all* of the business processes and systems impacted by the project, only a few. So if you concentrate initially on those difficult requirements and confine your explorations to the specific business processes and systems whose design they challenge, you will have a smaller number of smaller designs to explore. This will simplify your search for suitable designs. Since the remaining requirements are, by definition, easier to accommodate, addressing them will be less likely to require alterations to the design already established. In fact, it is most likely that whatever design you select to satisfy the challenging requirements will be readily extensible to support the less challenging requirements. This is the guiding principle behind Total Architecture Synthesis.

The Solution: Total Architecture Synthesis

TAS takes an iterative approach to the requirements gathering, business process synthesis, and architecture synthesis portions of the overall project lifecycle (Figure 9–2). It begins with an initial breadth-first

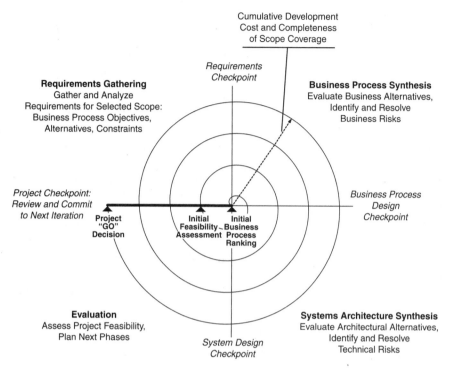

Figure 9–2: *Overview of Total Architecture Synthesis*

inventory of all the business processes that are in scope for the project. It ranks these business processes, grouped into use cases, by the anticipated level of design difficulty and business importance. Once the initial ranking is complete, the iterations begin. Each iteration is comprised of requirements gathering, business process synthesis, architecture synthesis, and a concluding evaluation.

In the first iteration, you select a small number of the most challenging business processes based on the ranking you have just completed. You gather the requirements for these business processes, including the expected results, benefits, and operating constraints. You next explore possible designs for the business process and select one or two promising designs for further exploration. You explore the architectural alternatives available to support the selected business process designs. You select one or two of these architectural alternatives and evaluate the selected business process and architecture designs to determine which, if any, can achieve the overall business benefit within the cost and schedule guidelines. If this assessment is favorable, you select the most promising of these business process and system designs as the basis for the next iteration. You then select the additional business processes to be considered in the next iteration and begin the next iteration.

If, on the other hand, you do not find a favorable evaluation after the initial iteration, you have not yet found a combination of business process and system design capable of producing the expected benefits within the cost and schedule guidelines. At this point, you need to pause and reconsider what you are doing. Although it is clearly appropriate to explore additional design alternatives, while doing so you should keep in mind the possibility that you may be looking at an infeasible project given the current cost and schedule guidelines.

If you reach the conclusion that your project is not feasible, at least within the current guidelines, the good news is that you have made this discovery with a minimal expenditure of effort and time. Furthermore, since the small amount of work you have done is focused entirely on the core feasibility questions, you have gained some insight as to exactly which requirements are presenting the challenge.

You can use this understanding to propose changes to the requirements, goals, schedule, and budget that would then yield a feasible project. The bad news concerning the project feasibility can then be accompanied by a proposal for altering the project charter. If these changes are not acceptable, the project oversight team may choose to abandon the project altogether and apply the resources to another project. Regardless of the outcome, you have reached this point with a minimum of time and resources and have therefore maximized the time and resources available to pursue other opportunities.

Figure 9–3 details the TAS approach. The process begins with the chartering of the project. The charter quantifies the expected benefits and the cost and schedule guidelines within which these benefits are to be achieved. I will discuss the details of the project charter in Chapter 11.

Project Scoping

TAS itself begins with an initial scoping of the project in terms of the business processes that will be impacted by the project. These processes are then grouped into use cases by commonality of business process result. The use cases are then ranked according to the anticipated level of design difficulty and business importance. In parallel, generic requirements that are not specific to the conduct of individual

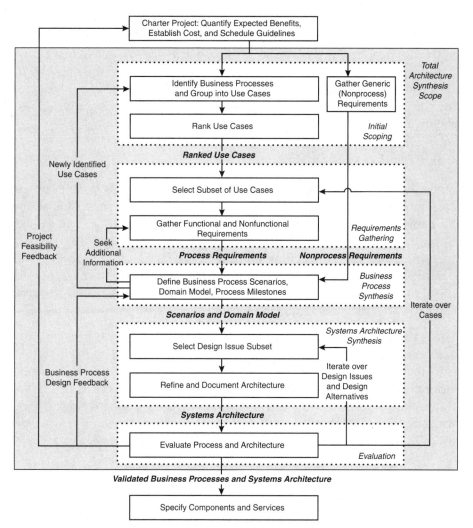

Figure 9–3: *Details of Total Architecture Synthesis*

business processes are gathered. These generic requirements will apply to all business processes in the inventory. This initial scoping process is discussed further in *SOA in Practice: Implementing Total Architecture,* the companion volume for this book.

Requirements Gathering

Once you have completed the initial scoping, you can begin the requirements gathering phase. You select a small number of use cases from the ranked list for the current iteration. On the first iteration, this may be just a single use case if there is one business process that dominates the project. Gather the requirements for the selected use cases, paying particular attention to identifying the required business process results, key performance indicators, and service-level agreements for the overall business process. The requirements to be gathered are detailed in the companion volume.

Business Process Synthesis

Once the requirements have been gathered, you begin business process synthesis—the actual design of the business processes. This activity explores the various business process alternatives that can be used to produce the required results and captures the business rules related to these processes. Particular emphasis is placed on identifying the participants in the proposed processes, their individual activities, and the communications between them. The information required to carry out each activity is also identified.

Some sources of required information may lie outside the current business process. In such cases, the business processes that produce this information and make it available to the business process being considered must also be identified. If these supporting business processes require modification and are not already in the use case inventory, they must be added. Note that such additions constitute a change in scope (or at least a growing awareness of the actual scope) for the project.

As these business processes and their alternatives are being defined, the key concepts and relationships involved in the processes are captured in a domain model. This model emphasizes the variability in relationships that can occur in the actual application domain and thus serves as a reference against which proposed data structure and schema representations can be evaluated. The business-meaningful milestones in the business process are also captured. These milestones must be clearly identifiable in the business process and system designs.

The explorations of business processes and the assemblage of the domain model and milestones may raise questions about requirements and thus require reengaging with the stakeholders to seek clarification. At the conclusion of business process synthesis, the risks and advantages of the different business process alternatives are explored, and one or two promising business process definitions are selected as input to the next step. The details of business process synthesis are discussed in the companion volume.

Systems Architecture Synthesis

Once the candidate business processes have been selected, you can begin the systems architecture synthesis, exploring the various system design alternatives that could support the selected business processes. In defining the architecture, you must address a number of design challenges. Rather than tackle them all at once, you can again take an iterative approach. Rank the design issues, and tackle them a few at a time. After refining each of the proposed architectural alternatives to address these issues, you evaluate the overall results. This evaluation weeds out unsuitable alternatives early in the game and singles out the best candidates. If suitable candidates are found, additional design issues are addressed. If no suitable alternatives are found, you must explore alternative architectures. However, you must once again keep your mind open to the possibility that there is no suitable architecture that will yield the desired benefits within the cost and schedule guidelines. The details of systems architecture synthesis are discussed in the companion volume.

Evaluation

As should be apparent from this discussion of TAS, evaluation is not necessarily a monolithic activity performed once in each cycle. Rather, it is an ongoing process that tests the suitability of business process and system designs as needed. As with the design issues in systems architecture synthesis, there are a number of evaluation questions to ask about the overall design. These questions are also ranked, with the showstopper questions such as performance feasibility placed high on the list. When the early design issues are being addressed, you consider only a few of the most fundamental evaluation questions.

As the design becomes more complete (with respect to the use cases being considered), you can answer more of these evaluation questions. At the end, however, there is really only one question to be answered: Does it still appear feasible to achieve the desired business benefit within the cost and schedule guidelines? If the answer is yes, it is time to move on with the design and consider more design issues or use cases. If the answer is no, it is time to engage the business executive sponsor and project oversight team to rethink the project.

Beware of Look-Alike Processes!

Iterative development processes and agile development have become quite popular in recent years. These techniques, and TAS as well, seek to reduce risk by trying out ideas quickly as a means of validating them and obtaining feedback. But I must urge some caution here. Agile development that attempts to produce a working system quickly often tackles the simplest aspects of a problem first. These aspects generally do not pose any particular architectural challenges. Consequently, in the early stages of the project, virtually any architecture may appear to be adequate. Yet if an inappropriate architecture is selected (by accident), by the time the difficult requirements are addressed, a considerable investment will have already been made in the inappropriate architecture. Changing the architecture at this point will be costly and time consuming—and may even be cost prohibitive. Whoops!

Barry Boehm sums the issue up nicely: "As in life, if you marry your architecture in haste, you and your stakeholders will repent at leisure."[2] Care should be taken to consciously select the architecture and evaluate its suitability before making a commitment to the architecture. As you are considering it, you should interpret architecture broadly as being inclusive of the business process design as well. Total Architecture Synthesis aims to do exactly this for the design of distributed information systems, testing and reviewing the design of both the business process and supporting systems on paper before committing to an implementation effort.

The use of Total Architecture Synthesis is not necessarily inconsistent with agile development methodologies that seek early implementations. At any point in the TAS iterative business process and architecture development, a subset of the business processes and supporting systems can be driven to implementation. However, to maintain risk at acceptable levels, it is imperative that even if the more difficult business processes and supporting systems are not implemented in these early iterations, they still have to be designed to avoid accidentally implementing an inappropriate architecture.

---

2. Barry Boehm, *Spiral Development: Experience, Principles, and Refinements* (2000), p. 15.

Manage Risk: Architect as You Go

A question we need to keep always in focus is whether the project is feasible. Can you actually deliver the expected project benefits within the cost and schedule guidelines? The question may be easy to ask, but it is hard to answer truthfully—especially when you are well into the project. The problem is that the further you are into the project, the greater the investment that has been made and the more difficult it becomes to report that the project (at least as chartered) is not feasible.

Generally, by the time you have finished the design work in a project, it is too late. Promises have been made, career reputations staked; money has been invested, critical time elapsed. But this problem is avoidable by restructuring the early phases of the work as just out-lined. Instead of making a large investment in requirements gathering followed by a large investment in architecture (the first point at which a definitive answer becomes possible), you focus instead on exploring only those business processes that are likely to pose a feasibility chal-lenge. By focusing on those business processes and their associated systems architecture, you can provide an early answer to the feasibility question with minimal investment.

Total Architecture Synthesis can thus be seen as a risk management technique. In fact, it is entirely appropriate to introduce a few project oversight team reviews and project go/no-go decisions into TAS's iter-ative cycles of expanding use case coverage. This gives the oversight team the opportunity to identify, at minimal cost, the projects whose unfolding costs or schedules are becoming inconsistent with project expectations. This early exposure affords maximum flexibility in terms of rescoping the project, increasing the budget, or reassigning the resources to more beneficial projects.

Total Architecture Synthesis provides an efficient means of attacking a business problem and delivering the desired benefits within cost and schedule guidelines. Its initial focus on the difficult aspects of a prob-lem leads to a quick determination as to whether these benefits are, indeed, achievable within the given constraints. This focus also leads to the efficient exploration of design alternatives and thus a lower-cost development process. It also ensures that both the business process and system designs are up to the task before the detailed specification of system components and services is undertaken. The use of UML standard notation creates documentation that enables a common understanding of both business process and system design that can be shared between the business and technical communities.

Summary

Traditional IT development methodologies do not adequately address enterprise-scale projects or interdependencies between business process design and systems design. Waterfall-style approaches assume that the resulting business process designs will permit reasonable system designs, while in reality some give-and-take is required to arrive at effective business processes with reasonable supporting system designs. Agile development does not address the multiple-organization challenge of enterprise projects, and it leads to an early commitment to an architecture before the challenging aspects of the problem have necessarily been addressed.

The Total Architecture Synthesis approach provides an effective alternative. Its iterative approach efficiently blends requirements gathering with business process and systems design and provides an early assessment of project feasibility. It quickly identifies the business processes that are most likely to present feasibility challenges and addresses them first. Business process by business process, it guides the architecture team through gathering requirements, designing the business process and supporting systems, and evaluating the design. Its evaluations provide both cost and performance feasibility assessments before a commitment is made to implementation. Its artifacts, based on industry-standard UML notation, promote efficient and effective cross-communication between the business process and systems communities. TAS keeps the project focused on delivering business value.

Key Project Lifecycle Questions

1. Does the business executive sponsor understand that project feasibility cannot be firmly established until some level of business process and system design has been performed and evaluated? How will the sponsor follow this ongoing feasibility evaluation?

2. What body of stakeholders will be the project checkpoint gatekeepers, deciding the business process scope for each iteration, reviewing the evaluation results at the end of the iteration, and making the decision as to whether or not to proceed with the next iteration? How is this process formalized?

Suggested Reading

Boehm, Barry. *Spiral Development: Experience, Principles, and Refinements*. Special Report CMU/SEI-2000-SR-008. Pittsburgh, PA: Carnegie Mellon University.

Part II

Managing Risk

Chapter 10

Responsibility and Risk in Business Processes

Breakdowns in business processes or systems pose risks for the enterprise, and undetected breakdowns pose even greater risks. This chapter explores the inner dialogs within business processes and the impacts they have on your ability to detect breakdowns and thus to manage risk.

Systems Can't Take Responsibility

The design of a business process defines how your enterprise operates on a day-to-day basis. When you consider this design, there is a natural tendency to focus on the normal executions of the business process. These sunny-day scenarios represent the majority of the business activity, and you certainly want their executions to be timely and efficient. However, you also need to consider the things that can go wrong with the process—both the expected and the unexpected. You want to ensure that your enterprise handles both in a manner that meets the business needs.

Let's start with an apparently philosophical question: Can systems really take responsibility? As we involve computers more deeply in managing and monitoring business processes, it is natural for us to want computers to take on some of the burden of responsibility as well. However, systems cannot really take on responsibility in the same sense that people can. Winograd and Flores observe that systems cannot be committed to getting the job done with the same type of flexibility as people.[1] Systems can neither assess risks nor take responsibility for consequences. Only people can do these things.

This has significant practical implications for the design of systems. If systems cannot take on a responsibility, you need to understand who really owns that responsibility. It is these people who must assess risks, respond to unusual circumstances, and take responsibility for consequences. These considerations have a profound influence on the design of both the business processes and the systems that support them.

So why can't systems take on responsibility? To answer this question, you first need to understand what it means for a person to take on a responsibility. When you ask someone to perform a task, you are in effect asking him or her to take on the responsibility for performing that task. In accepting this responsibility, the person is making a *commitment* to do whatever is necessary to get the task done (within reason, of course). This commitment extends to performing the task *even under unexpected circumstances*. In this regard, a system cannot truly take responsibility. Systems simply do not have the flexibility to handle unexpected situations. They can respond only to situations for which they were programmed. Consequently, if you want your business processes and systems to handle unexpected situations gracefully, you must design them to engage people when these unexpected situations arise.

The implications are that you must design your systems to both identify unusual circumstances *and communicate their existence to the people responsible for the proper execution of the business process*. Breakdowns in business processes—the failure of an activity to produce its expected results in a timely manner—are important indicators of unexpected situations. Many real-world business process disruptions occur because the systems are not designed to detect these breakdowns and alert people.

---

1. Terry Winograd and Fernando Flores, *Understanding Computers and Cognition: A New Foundation for Design* (1986).

Chapter 2 presented a classic example of this, describing how purchase requests went missing for days before anybody noticed. You cannot, by definition, design for the unexpected. However, you *can* do the opposite. You can monitor to see whether the expected is actually happening and in a timely manner. You can design the systems to do this monitoring and report any exceptions. Then, if you add an appropriate "people system" to respond to the exceptions, you will have a business process capable of handling the unexpected.

Your design for handling the unexpected must extend beyond simply reporting the exceptions. You also have to consider the actions that people will take in diagnosing and recovering from the breakdowns. These activities may involve additional interactions with systems involving different functionality and interfaces than the sunny-day scenarios. Thus, an understanding of these diagnostic and recovery procedures is required to complete the design of the system.

Of course, before you can handle a breakdown, you first need to know that one has occurred. You need to know that the process has stopped executing normally. How can you determine this? I will begin answering this question by examining a simple dialog between two people in which one asks the other to perform a task. In this examination, I will pay particular attention to the individual communications between the participants and the roles they play in the detection of breakdowns, and I will then consider how this dialog changes when one or both of the participants become systems. It will become clear how your system designs can be modified to detect breakdowns and engage humans when the unexpected occurs. These modifications will enable you to bring the flexibility of human response back into the business process, even when there is heavy systems involvement. Along the way, you will also see how some common communications shortcuts literally make it impossible to detect breakdowns.

The Conversation for Action

Let's consider how people go about delegating a task; we'll look specifically at the conversation between the individuals involved. Winograd and Flores[2] have formulated an elegantly simple model of this

2. Winograd and Flores, *Understanding Computers and Cognition.*

dialog they call the *conversation for action*. Figure 10–1 shows an overview of this dialog, represented in UML collaboration diagram notation. The dialog begins when one person (whom we will call the `Requestor`) asks another person (whom we will call the `Performer`) to perform some task. For example, if you have a plumbing problem, you might call a plumber and leave a message asking him to come and fix the problem.

This communication is a *request*. The `Performer`, if he accepts the request, responds with a *promise* to perform the task. In this example, the plumber returns your call, and you arrange a visit from the plumber. In other words, the plumber promises to do the work. Some time later, the `Performer` actually performs the task and makes the *result* of the task available to the `Requestor` (or at least announces the completion of the task). In this example, the plumber comes and does the work and at some point indicates to you that the repair is complete. Finally, the `Requestor` evaluates the result and provides *feedback* about the result to the `Performer`. In this example, you evaluate the plumbing repair and, if you are satisfied, you pay the plumber and thus accept the work.

This conversation is just a sunny-day scenario. An actual conversation can be much more complex. Figure 10–2, using the notation of a UML state diagram, shows the states of the dialog and transitions between them associated with some common variations. For compactness, I have used R and P in the diagram to identify the actions of the `Requestor` and `Performer`, respectively. The states of the basic conversation are shaded. After the `Requestor` makes the initial request, a number of things might happen other than the `Performer` simply returning a promise. The `Requestor` might choose to withdraw the request (you might decide to fix the plumbing problem yourself), or

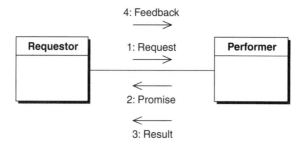

Figure 10–1: *Overview of the Conversation for Action*

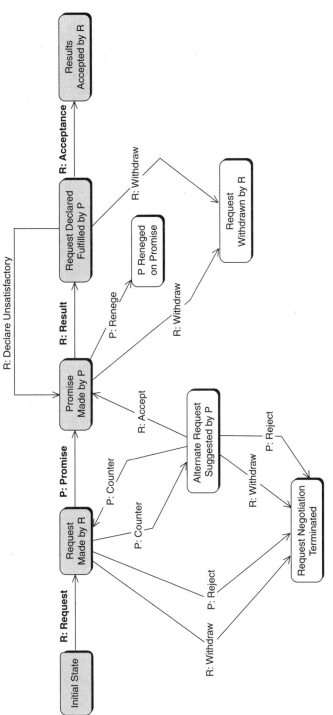

Figure 10–2: *State Model of the Basic Conversation for Action*

the `Performer` might reject the request (the plumber does not have time for your job). The two parties might negotiate the definition of the task. The `Performer` might counter by proposing some alternative (the plumber might suggest an alternate time to effect the repair or suggest replacing rather than repairing the broken fixture). Once the proposal has been made, the `Requestor` might accept the proposed alternative, make a counter suggestion (you propose yet another time), or withdraw the request altogether (you decide to fix it yourself or call a different plumber).

Once an agreement is reached and a promise made, there are again a number of things that might happen. The `Performer` might renege on the promise (the plumber may not show up), or the `Requestor` might withdraw the request (you cancel the appointment). Once the work has been performed and the results delivered, still other possibilities emerge. The `Requestor` might reject the results (you decide the repair was unsatisfactory and refuse to pay) or withdraw the request altogether (although this may carry with it some penalty at this stage). The possible variations in this dialog are nearly endless.

With all this variability, you can begin to see some of the limitations of making a system one of the participants in the dialog. While people may be able to deal with this almost boundless variety, systems cannot. In order for a system to participate in the dialog in either role, all of the expected dialog variations that it is supposed to handle must be clearly defined. *More important, you have to recognize that if a system gets a response that does not fit the planned dialog, it cannot handle that response.*

The only possible action a system can take in response to the unexpected is to annunciate the fact that an unexpected situation has occurred. If you want your business process to be flexible, the design of that business process must include this annunciation and the response of the people required to resolve the situation.

Designing business processes and systems to handle the unexpected requires significant attention as the business processes and systems are being architected. If you do not accurately capture the normally expected dialog variations at design time, the result will be additional unexpected situation announcements from the systems at runtime. Incomplete requirements will also place the systems architect in the position of having to guess what the appropriate responses should be for different inputs. Incorrect guesses will result in even more unexpected situations for other systems.

Delegation and Trust

I have been talking about how one participant might ask another to perform a task or service but have not considered why. So why would you delegate a task to someone else? You delegate a task when you conclude that, for some specific reason, the task would be performed more appropriately by another participant. You then ask that participant to perform this service for you.

Two major expectations accompany this decision. One is that, when all is said and done, using the service will require less work on your part than if you did the work yourself. The other is one of trust: You trust the `Performer` to do the work. For example, you call a plumber when you conclude that (a) having the plumber do the job would involve less of your time and money than doing the job yourself, and (b) the plumber will do a quality job on time and at the quoted price.

But what is trust? Trust is the making and honoring of *commitments*. More specifically, when you delegate, you trust that the `Performer` (a) has the knowledge and skills required to carry out the responsibility, (b) is sincere in taking on the responsibility (i.e., has no conflicting agendas that might compromise the commitment to discharge the responsibility), and (c) has the available capacity to actually do the job within the requested time frame.[3] You also trust that the `Performer` will, within reason, adapt to unexpected situations that arise in attempting to execute the task. If all of these conditions are not met, the `Performer` will not execute the task in the manner that you expect.

Using services makes little sense unless there is both a net savings in work effort on the part of the `Requestor` and a corresponding level of trust in the `Performer`. In the plumbing example, you expect that it will require less work on your part to retain the plumber than it would to make the repair yourself. In addition, you trust that the plumber knows how to do the work, is sincere in agreeing to do the work (i.e., is not just accepting the job to keep a competitor from getting the work), and actually has the time and resources to come and fix your problem as promised. In casual interactions, it is the `Requestor`'s responsibility to not only manage the use of the service but also determine that the delegation is, in fact, appropriate.

---

3. An extensive exploration of the concept of trust can be found in Robert C. Solomon and Fernando Flores, *Building Trust: In Business, Politics, Relationships, and Life* (2001).

Tying this discussion back to the earlier one about the limitations of systems, consider the implications of the `Performer` being a system. Who, exactly, are you trusting here? If you think about it for a while, you will conclude that you are not trusting the system—you are trusting the people responsible for the design and operation of that system. It is the people who embed the knowledge and skills in the design of the system. It is the people who are sincere about putting that system into service. It is the people who provide the system capacity needed to perform the service. And it is the people who must cope with the unexpected situations. You don't trust systems, you trust people.

When you are designing a business process, the determination of which tasks ought to be delegated to which participants is an architectural responsibility. You have to appreciate the extent to which the business process and systems architects are not only making decisions to trust the various organizations to do their part but also asking those organizations to commit to performing those delegated tasks, both at design time and at runtime.

The architects cannot make these commitments. All they can really do is determine an assignment of tasks that will provide a workable business process and then seek the commitment of the organizations involved to execute those tasks. This involves design-time commitments to alter systems and runtime commitments to perform manual tasks, operate systems, and resolve breakdowns. Once again, you see the importance of aligning organizational priorities with those of the project. Without such alignment, the architects will not be able to obtain the necessary commitments. Only the business executive sponsor and IT executive sponsor are in a position to align priorities by establishing organizational performance measurements, incentive compensation schemes, and budgets.

Detecting Breakdowns in Task Performance

Return now to the task delegation dialog, and reexamine it with an eye toward identifying breakdowns in the performance of the task. This time, I represent the conversation as a UML activity diagram, a notation I will use extensively in modeling processes at both the business and systems levels in *SOA in Practice: Implementing Total Architecture*,

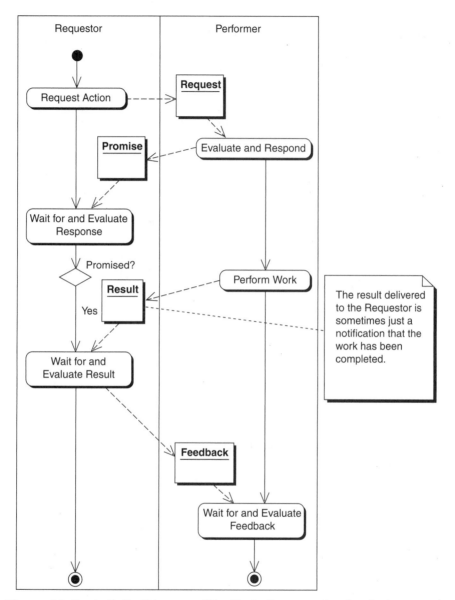

Figure 10–3: *Activity Diagram of the Basic Conversation for Action*

the companion volume to this book. Figure 10–3 uses this notation to present the basic conversation for action—a sunny-day walk down the shaded path shown in Figure 10–2.

UML Activity Diagram Notation

The UML activity diagram notation is basically a flowchart extended to indicate which process participant is performing each of the activities. Each participant is represented as a column called a swimlane. Each activity is shown as a rounded rectangle. The placement of an activity in a swimlane indicates that the participant represented by the swimlane is responsible for performing that activity.

The solid arrows between activities represent the sequencing of activities. Communications between participants are represented by showing exactly what is communicated (e.g., a message, file, or database record) between the participants. The communicated object is represented by a rectangle. An arrow from an activity to an object indicates that this activity generated the object, and arrows from the object to other activities indicate that these activities consume the object. Unlike the placement of activities in swimlanes, the placement of an object within a swimlane has no significance.

Notes (icons that look like pieces of paper with the corner folded) can be added to annotate the diagram, and dotted lines can connect the notes to the diagram elements to which they refer.

Awaiting the Promise

Walking through this dialog from the Requestor's perspective, you should pay particular attention to activities that can aid you in determining whether or not the process is executing properly. The process begins with the Requestor formulating a request, submitting it to the Performer, and then waiting for a response. In the sunny-day scenario, you expect this response to be a promise. Of course, the actual response must be examined to determine whether it is, indeed, the expected promise instead of some other unexpected response. This activity, waiting for and evaluating the response, is a key monitoring point for the Requestor.

But what if there is no response? Is this lack of response a problem? The answer is—maybe! This is not a particularly useful answer, of course, as you would like to be able to treat the absence of a response as an indication of a breakdown in the process. However, you also must expect there to be some normal delay before you receive a response. The problem you have in interpreting the absence of a response is that you have not established a required time frame for providing the response. Phrased in a more conventional way, you have not established a service-level agreement regarding the timing of the response. *In the absence of an established time frame, you cannot meaningfully interpret the lack of a response.*

You can see the side effects of ill-defined response times in everyday conversation. If someone is engrossed in a task and you ask a question, you may not get an immediate response. Under these circumstances, it is unclear whether (a) the person is so deeply engrossed that he or she did not hear the request; (b) the person heard the request but has not yet reached a point in the task where he or she can reasonably break concentration and reply without disrupting the task; or (c) the person actually gave a reply, but in a manner that you did not recognize (a nod, a gesture, or a grunt of acknowledgment). For all you know, the person might have decided to simply ignore the request!

The dilemma you face in such situations is that while conversational convention dictates that the recipient of a question should respond soon after the question is asked, there is no precise definition of "soon." The absence of a well-defined response time thus creates an inherent ambiguity in the absence of a response. In conversation, we deal with this ambiguity by waiting what we believe to be a reasonable period of time and then asking the question again, perhaps in a more forceful manner. Our personal judgment also impacts our behavior. If the task the person is engaged in appears to be critical, we might wait longer before interrupting again. And, once again, our human flexibility in responding to the unexpected comes into play.

From this discussion, you can conclude that if you want to definitively interpret the absence of a response, you must first establish the time frame within which the response is to be expected. This gives rise to a common best practice when giving work assignments: In addition to clearly indicating what the task is, you also indicate when you expect the task to be completed. This is tantamount to establishing a service-level agreement.

When one of the participants in the dialog is a system, establishing this service-level agreement regarding the allowed response time is absolutely essential. Without it, the system has no basis for interpreting the absence of a response. If the `Performer` is a system, meeting this service-level agreement becomes a design requirement. In the absence of a specified requirement, the designer of the performing system can only guess as to what kind of response time is acceptable, and this guess may not be consistent with the `Requestor`'s expectations. Conversely, if the `Requestor` is a system, establishing the response time in the service-level agreement makes it possible for the system to distinguish between an expected delay and a true breakdown. *You conclude then that the establishment of a service-level agreement governing the allowed time frame for a response is an essential element in detecting breakdowns, particularly when systems are involved.*

Monitoring and evaluating responses can tell a lot about the health of the process up to that point. While a number of possible breakdowns can occur prior to the activity that awaits the response, any prior breakdown can be detected by this activity. The request might have been lost. The request might not have been understood by the `Performer`, which resulted in either the request being ignored or a response seeking clarification. The `Performer` might have understood the request but, for any number of reasons, not responded. Or the response itself might have been lost in transit. All of these breakdowns will result in either a no-response situation or a response indicating a problem. Thus, with a dialog design that includes an explicit acceptance within the response and an established service-level agreement governing the response time, the `Performer` can definitively establish the health of the overall process up to that point.

Awaiting the Result

After receiving the initial response (assuming that the response was a promise), the `Requestor` continues to wait for the anticipated results. This is another key process monitoring point. The absence of the result may be an indication of a breakdown in either the performance of the work or the delivery of the result. As with the promise, the absence of a result cannot be interpreted if a time frame for receiving the result has not been established. A second service-level agreement is required. In addition, the result itself must contain sufficient information that it can be evaluated. Evaluation is important for status monitoring. A misunderstanding on the part of the `Performer` might result in an improper result being generated, and this will not become apparent until the results are evaluated. When there is a service-level agreement in place, this monitor-and-evaluate activity can detect any breakdown in the process (save for a breakdown of the `Requestor` itself) from the point at which the initial request was submitted up to the point at which the result is expected.

Evaluating the Request

Looking at this dialog from the `Performer`'s perspective, you can see that the `Performer` is also in a position to detect breakdowns. The evaluate-and-respond activity is the first monitoring point for the `Performer`. Although a lost request cannot be detected (the `Performer` has no idea that a request was sent), an ill-formed request can be identified by evaluating the request. If both participants are people, such situations can be rectified through further dialog. However, if either participant is a system, the only recourse is for the `Performer` to announce the existence of a problem by simply rejecting the request.

Awaiting the Feedback

The wait-for-and-evaluate-feedback activity is the other `Performer` monitoring point. For meaningful breakdown detection, this activity depends on an established service-level agreement regarding the timing of the feedback once the result has been delivered. A number of breakdowns in the process will result in the absence of this feedback. The result might have been lost on its way to the `Requestor`, there might have been a breakdown in the `Requestor`'s evaluation, or the feedback itself might have been lost.

For effective monitoring, the feedback must contain more than a simple acknowledgment of the results receipt. It must contain the `Requestor`'s conclusion drawn from evaluating those results. If this information is included, waiting for and evaluating the feedback provides an opportunity for the `Performer` to recognize any breakdown after the receipt of the initial request, including an incorrectly interpreted request, improperly performed work, and a lost result. Here I must note yet another system limitation: While a person might be able to constructively respond to negative feedback, all a system can really do is bring it to human attention. The people responsible for the system are the only ones who can take action to correct the situation.

Systems as Participants

In summary, you can see that the conversation for action provides many opportunities for both the `Requestor` and `Performer` to detect breakdowns in the process. For this breakdown detection to be effective, service-level agreements governing the time frames for all expected communications must be established, including the promise, result, and feedback. For complete breakdown detection, the promise, result, and feedback must be more than simple acknowledgments—they must provide evaluation results as well. If all of these conditions are met, and all four monitoring points are actively checking for communications and evaluating the results, virtually all breakdowns in the process can be reliably detected. The only combination of failures that will go undetected is the loss of the request coupled with the subsequent loss of the `Requestor`.

Since systems are limited in their ability to handle unexpected situations, when systems participate in the dialog, each system must have personnel responsible for handling the unexpected situations faced by that system. These are the support people who respond to system exception reports. Furthermore, each system must be explicitly designed to alert its operators when exceptions occur. If we do these things, the result is the extended dialog shown in Figure 10–4. Not shown in the figure, but absolutely essential to the successful execution of the process, are the recovery actions performed by the operations and support personnel in response to these exceptions.

Dialog Shortcuts Increase Risk

Even though this dialog is somewhat simplistic, it is comprehensive in its lifecycle coverage of a service request. In real life, however, you often take shortcuts in the things you do, and this is true for service request dialogs as well. While taking a shortcut is generally motivated by a desire to save work and time, you have to recognize that taking a shortcut also entails a measure of risk. This is particularly true for the conversation for action.

When you omit portions of the task management dialog, you give up the ability to detect some of the breakdowns that can occur. The resulting risk is that the larger process, of which this task-related dialog is but a portion, will be disrupted in some unexpected and unplanned-for way. In this section, I will explore how specific omissions in the dialog impact your ability to detect breakdowns. I will look first at omitting single interactions and then at what happens when you omit all the dialog except the initial request. *While such a large-scale omission may seem odd in light of the discussion I have just completed, this pattern is actually the most common type of system-to-system interaction, despite its being the riskiest of all the options!*

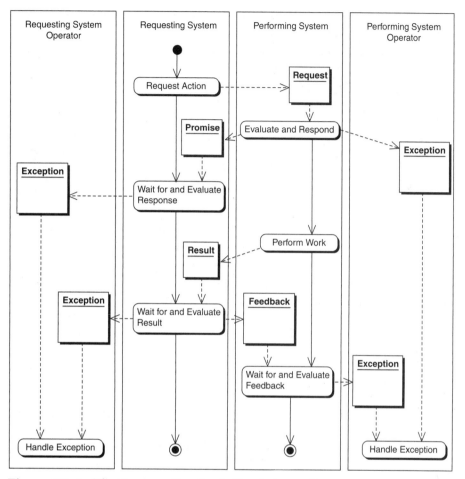

Figure 10–4: *The Conversation for Action between Systems*

Omitting the Promise

The promise serves the purpose of letting the `Requestor` know that the `Performer` has received the request and has agreed to perform the task. Omitting the promise is common when you expect the result immediately. For example, when you ask a question for which you expect an immediate answer, you do not expect a promise, you expect the answer. Such omissions are also common when there is a high level of confidence that the request will successfully reach the `Performer` and that the `Performer` will accept the responsibility and execute the task. For example, when you get your phone bill in the mail, you don't respond with a promise to pay, you send the payment.

The only real consequence of omitting the promise is that breakdowns will remain undetected until such time as the result is due, and thus recovery actions cannot begin until the result is overdue. The risk to the overall process is that should a breakdown occur, the task result is guaranteed to be late. The risks of omitting the promise are the consequences of delay for the larger process. In the case of your phone bill, if the bill is lost in the mail, the loss will likely not be discovered until the payment is overdue. The recovery action is that the phone company includes the overdue amount in the following month's bill. The risks are that the phone company's cash flow is impacted, and you may be subject to a late payment fee with a corresponding impact on your credit rating.

In systems design, it is common practice to omit the promise when you invoke a service using synchronous request-reply. For example, when a user submits a query and waits for the response, the responding system does not return a promise, it returns the query result. Since the `Requestor` is waiting for the result and expects it almost immediately, there is little point in sending a promise. On the other hand, when the reply will be delivered asynchronously, it is not at all uncommon for a promise to be returned. For example, when you order goods online, you receive an immediate order confirmation. This confirmation is the promise to deliver the goods.

A word of caution is in order here: A simple receipt acknowledgment is not the same thing as a promise. If you order goods via the mail and request a delivery receipt, that receipt simply indicates that the request was delivered. It does not indicate that the company understood your order, accepted your form of payment, has the goods available, and intends to ship them to you. Similarly, a simple message receipt acknowledgment in a system-to-system interaction does not indicate that the receiving system successfully acted on the message. Receipts should not be interpreted as promises.

Omitting the Feedback

Feedback is the mechanism for letting the `Performer` know whether or not the task was performed in a satisfactory manner. A common shortcut is to omit the feedback from the dialog. In the workplace, for example, we routinely omit the feedback when the work is satisfactory, providing feedback only when the work is wholly unsatisfactory. For example, an analyst working in an investment bank might be tasked with routinely tracking and reporting on a group of companies. The analyst produces these reports on a regular basis but neither expects nor receives any feedback about individual reports unless someone is unhappy with the results.

The risks associated with omitting the feedback are largely related to quality and the impact that quality has on the overall business process. Quality typically has a range associated with it. At the extremes, the results are either clearly acceptable or not acceptable. In between, however, there is usually a grey area. In this area, the results might not be as good as you would like them to be, but they are at least minimally acceptable. What you choose to do with these grey-area results can have a cumulative effect on your business processes.

Economy is the ostensible motivation for omitting this feedback. However, the reduction in design and operational costs associated with the omission may actually represent a false economy. The savings may be more than offset by the cumulative impact of marginal work.

If you deliver feedback only when work is wholly unsatisfactory (i.e., you accept grey-area results), the absence of negative feedback is often taken by the `Performer` to be an implicit indication that the results are wholly satisfactory. This interpretation is obviously incorrect when grey-area results have been accepted. The absence of feedback also deprives the `Performer` of the opportunity to learn from the feedback and take steps to improve future work.

The absence of negative feedback regarding grey-area results can have a snowball effect. If many tasks are performed with marginally acceptable results, the situation can build to a rather unpleasant climax in which the accumulated negative feedback is finally delivered, all at once, to the `Performer`. This communication might be triggered by the creation of one particularly poor result or might be delivered during an annual performance review. At this point, the `Performer` is finally told that the quality of work, in general, has been less than satisfactory. In the worst case, the `Performer` may be fired.

The cumulative effects of omitting feedback have caused an evolution in management best practices, which now encourage the active use of feedback. Williams observes that "Continuous feedback gives the employee the opportunity to adjust behavior as he or she goes along."[4]

---

4. Monci J. Williams, "Performance Appraisal Is Dead. Long Live Performance Management!" *Harvard Management Update*, 2(2), February 1997.

Failing that, Williams notes, "Advocates of the new performance management systems suggest that managers have three or four performance-related conversations with each direct report in the course of the year."

Feedback that includes quality measurements can be used for much more than just refining an individual `Performer`'s skills. It can be used to guide overall process quality as well. Six Sigma and other product quality control approaches continually monitor the quality of manufacturing process results. These quality measurements are then used to guide the evolutionary improvement of the manufacturing process. These improvements, in turn, reduce the number of defective products. In the Six Sigma approach, the goal is to reduce defects to less than 3.4 per million, which is six standard deviations (six sigma) from the mean. In manufacturing, this is an approach to increasing customer satisfaction and thus increasing sales and profitability.

This principle of measuring the aspect of a process we are trying to improve is central to achieving business results in general. If you aren't defining measurable success criteria and measuring your progress toward achieving success, you don't really know whether you are being successful. Feedback containing these measurements is an essential element of process improvement.

While it is obvious how feedback causes changes when the `Performer` is a person, it should be equally obvious that a system cannot, by itself, act on such feedback. It is the personnel responsible for the system who are in a position to do something constructive with the feedback. These people can evaluate the feedback and determine the system changes that need to be made to avoid whatever problems have arisen or to improve the quality of results. In order for these people to respond to the feedback, however, they must first receive the feedback and then act on it. Receiving the feedback involves systems design, and responding to the feedback involves business process design.

Let's consider the systems design associated with delivering this feedback. There are two basic patterns we can use. The first is illustrated in Figure 10–5. Here the `Requesting System` evaluates the result and determines whether or not it is acceptable. Unacceptable results are annunciated to the people operating this system, and these people take the initiative to notify the owners of the `Performing System` that there is a problem.

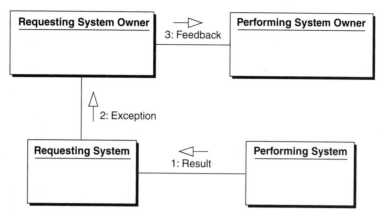

Figure 10–5: *Feedback Involving Systems—Pattern 1*

The second feedback pattern is illustrated in Figure 10–6. Here the `Requesting System` evaluates the result and sends the exception indicating a bad result back to the `Performing System`. The `Performing System`, in turn, notifies the people responsible for the system that there is a problem. This pattern involves more systems design work than the first pattern. In either case, the feedback must eventually reach the personnel responsible for the `Performing System` and be acted on in order for the feedback to have any effect.

The evaluation and feedback regarding results are critical to business process quality. Business process architects need to be consciously aware of the role that the evaluation and feedback play and of the consequences of their omissions. While such omissions may reduce both

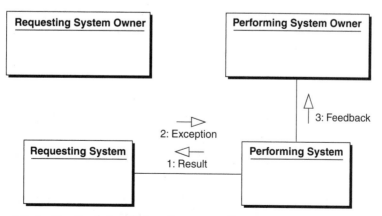

Figure 10–6: *Feedback Involving Systems—Pattern 2*

the level of effort required to build the business process and support-ing systems and the apparent required size of the operations staff, they also increase the risk to the enterprise arising from poor-quality results. Such omissions leave the enterprise in the dark about quality and should generally be avoided.

When systems are involved, evaluating work results and providing feedback require explicit design activity, both at the systems level and at the business process level. At the systems level, the criteria for estab-lishing the acceptability of a result must be specified, and the actual check for acceptability must be implemented. The mechanism for bringing exceptions to the attention of the operations personnel must also be designed and implemented. At the business process level, the process for responding to these announcements must also be designed, particularly if the work in progress is to be fixed.

Omitting the Results

Omit the results? While this may sound ludicrous, what often happens in practice is that the results are not sent back to the `Requestor` but are sent to a `Third Party` instead (Figure 10–7). When this occurs, the `Requestor` no longer expects any results and thus is no longer in a posi-tion either to determine whether the results were generated or to evaluate the results. The results evaluation responsibility thus must be borne by the `Third Party`, who then provides feedback to the `Performer`.

You can see this pattern when you order flowers and have them sent to someone. You see it when you send a donation to a charitable organi-zation that promises to use it to provide some sort of aid. Since the flowers and the aid are not delivered to you, you have no way to deter-mine whether the task was actually performed (unless you get a thank-you from the person who received the flowers!). The risk of this type of omission is that breakdowns in the performance of the task will result in completely undetected breakdowns in the overall process.

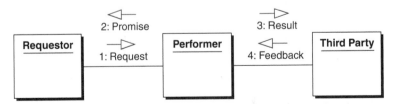

Figure 10–7: *Delivering Results to a Third Party*

If the feedback is omitted as well, you now have a situation in which none of the participants is in a position to detect any breakdown in the process after the promise. The consequence is that breakdowns will become evident only when the absence of the result causes a problem in the larger process. This can happen when you have equipment drop-shipped to a customer site. You order the equipment and give instructions to the supplier (the `Performer`) to ship it to the customer site so that it will be there when we need it. However, if there is a breakdown in this process, you will not be aware of it until after you arrive at the site and want to use the equipment.

You can also add communications to make third-party delivery more robust. If you still require the feedback, and furthermore have the `Performer` send a notification to the `Requestor` on receipt of the feedback, then the `Requestor` is in a position to determine that the overall result has been delivered and accepted by the `Third Party` (Figure 10–8). Note that in order to catch all the possible breakdowns in the process, the notification cannot be sent to the `Requestor` until the feedback is received from the `Third Party`.

A different type of modification is to introduce another participant into the process whose sole purpose is to monitor the overall process (Figure 10–9). The `Monitor` receives notification of all major events in the dialog, specifically the generation of the initial request, a notification that the results have been created, and the feedback about the results. This puts the `Monitor` in a position to detect breakdowns in the dialog. However, it also introduces some new breakdown possibilities. For example, if the `Monitor` does not receive the initial request notification, the `Monitor` will not be in a position to detect the subsequent absence of the results or feedback communications. If this failure scenario sounds a bit pathological, consider that a single breakdown in the communications infrastructure could easily cause both the request and the request notification to be lost.

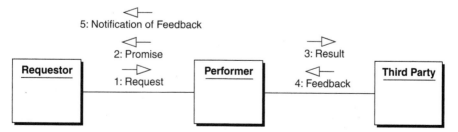

Figure 10–8: *Delivering Results to a Third Party with Notification*

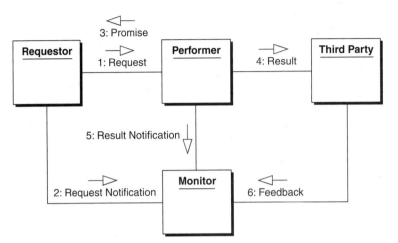

Figure 10–9: *Delivering Results to a Third Party with Monitoring*

Request-Only Interactions

If you omit the promise, results, and feedback, you are left with just the request (Figure 10–10). This pattern cannot detect any breakdowns whatsoever. Given this limitation, it might seem ludicrous that you would even consider it. But consider it you must, for despite its limitations, it is widely used. You see it in broadcast communications, where the request is an advertisement to purchase a product. You see it when someone yells, "Fire!" in a theater, where the request is an implicit plea to evacuate the premises. *Unfortunately, you will see it all too often in systems, where request-only (often referred to as fire-and-forget) communications are the most common form of interaction between systems!*

The motivation behind request-only dialogs is essentially economy. Broadcast advertising is relatively inexpensive. When there is a fire, it is time we are trying to economize when we yell, "Fire!" In systems development, it is generally development cost being economized. But such omissions are obviously accompanied by risks.

Figure 10–10: *Request-Only Interaction*

Because there is no confirming communication in a request-only inter-action, there is no direct means of determining whether or not there has been a breakdown in the process. Depending on the importance of the requested task, independent follow-up actions may be required on the part of the `Requestor` to assess the extent to which the request was successful. Surveys of consumers or an analysis of purchasing behavior can be used to establish whether or not the advertisement reached the audience and triggered the desired behavior. When a radio broadcast of an emergency evacuation order occurs, it is usually fol-lowed up with police and fire personnel canvassing the neighborhood to enforce the order. The very fact that such follow-up steps are com-monplace is a tacit acknowledgment of the breakdowns that can occur in these one-way communications. When the request is important, some form of confirmation is always required.

The business consequences of undetected breakdowns must be a major consideration when using request-only interactions in business processes. Consider the order-to-cash business process shown in Fig-ure 10–11. The handoff between the `Order Management` process and the `Warehouse Management` process in this diagram is a request-only interaction, with the released sales order comprising the request. If that sales order does not make it, or if there are problems in the `Warehouse Management` process itself, the `Order Management` pro-cess is not in a position to identify that a breakdown has occurred. As this process is shown, only the `Customer` will know that the order was not successfully processed.

While request-only interactions are simple to implement, the absence of feedback renders the detection of breakdowns impossible. Thus, the use of request-only interactions, or any of the other shortcut variations we have discussed, must be carefully evaluated in the context of the overall business process. Very often you will find that relatively minor variations in the business process can significantly reduce the risks. For example, if the process shown in Figure 10–11 were modified to simply send a copy of the shipment manifest to the `Order Management` system, this would put the `Order Management` system in a position to identify late shipments, i.e., breakdowns in the `Warehouse Management` process. I discuss these interaction patterns along with the larger-scale issues of business process monitoring and management in the com-panion volume.

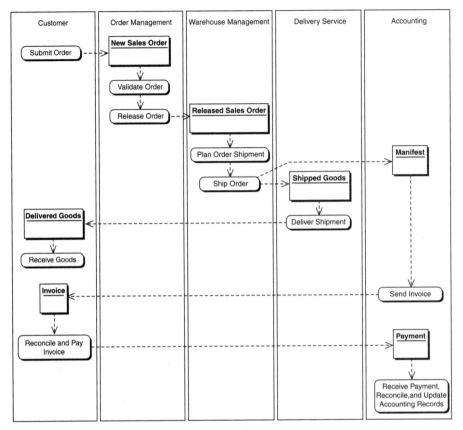

Figure 10–11: *Order-to-Cash Business Process*

Process Design and Responsibility Assignments

Discussion to this point has focused on a single task and the responsibilities of the `Requestor` and `Performer` with respect to executing that task. When the business process and systems architects design a business process, they are doing more than just determining the sequence of tasks required to produce the required results. They are also assigning these task-related responsibilities to the participants in the process.

Let's take a look at business process design from the perspective of the business process and systems architects. Our goal is to clarify implicit responsibility assignments that are being made as part of this design, so that both the architects and the participants clearly understand what those responsibilities are. This is particularly important when systems are involved, as some of these responsibilities end up being borne by operations and support personnel—people who are not direct participants in the day-to-day business process execution.

Business process design entails a number of design activities for the architects. Broadly, these activities are the following:

1. Designing the basic process flow
2. Establishing task performance constraints
3. Assigning task execution and management responsibilities
4. Assigning process monitoring and management responsibilities
5. Assigning results validation responsibilities

You should examine these design activities with an eye toward understanding who owns which responsibilities. In the ensuing discussion, I will use the generic term *architects* to refer to both business process and systems architects. This is because both participate in making responsibility assignments. The business process architect determines the responsibilities of people and of the systems taken as a whole. The systems architect takes the overall systems responsibilities and assigns them to individual components within the system. The two architects work together to determine which responsibilities are appropriate for people and which for systems.

Designing the Basic Process Flow

A process is a structured sequence of tasks that achieves a result. The architects' first design activity is to define this sequence of tasks. This includes the specification of any branching logic required to determine, at runtime, exactly which tasks need to be performed. I should note that this immediately brings the handling of exceptions into play. The architects need to determine which exceptions will have designed responses and which will lead to a find-the-problem-and-fix-it activity that can be assigned only to a person, not a system.

The need for this process design activity is obvious when the business process is new and the requirements have specified only *what* needs to be done and not *how*. The need for process design is somewhat less obvious when the process already exists and you are just modifying the process. Nevertheless, the need remains to ensure that the revised business process will, indeed, produce the expected results and business benefits.

The result of this design activity is an understanding of the various task sequences required to produce the results.

Establishing Task Performance Constraints

Business processes usually have constraints on their performance, often referred to as nonfunctional requirements. A common example is a response-time requirement specifying the maximum allowed time interval between the initiation of the process (e.g., the submission of a request) and the production of a result (e.g., the receipt of the response).

When you have such overall business process requirements, you need to determine what the corresponding requirements are for the individual tasks that comprise the business process. For the most part, this requires translating individual process constraints into individual task constraints. Consider once again the order-to-cash process shown earlier in Figure 10–11. Assume that the process constraints are that shipment must occur within 24 hours of receipt of the order, with the average order consisting of two items and the peak order rate being 100,000 orders per day. What does this mean for the individual tasks?

The first thing the architects have to do is establish a time budget for the individual tasks. If you have 24 hours to ship the product, you might allocate 2 hours to the complete Order Management process for credit checks and approvals and 22 hours for the Warehouse Management process. Within the Warehouse Management process, you might allocate 2 hours for the Plan Order Shipment task and 20 hours for the Ship Order task.

The architect also needs to determine the throughput requirements for each task—a first step toward capacity planning. If the warehouse operates only on a single-shift basis, the Ship Order task must be able to pack and ship 100,000 orders during the shift, each consisting of an average of two items.

Things can get more complicated if activity rates vary throughout the day. Consider what the process requirements would be if the shipment planning occurs as part of the single-shift warehouse operation, and furthermore the bulk of the orders are received at the end of the business day. In order to meet the 24-hour shipment guarantee, the Plan Order Shipment task would have to process all 100,000 orders in 2 hours, and the Ship Order task would have to process all of these orders in 6 remaining single-shift hours.

From this discussion, it should be obvious that there are a variety of ways in which the overall business process goals might be met. It is the job of the architects to determine the specific manner in which the goals will be met. The architects must determine the specific combination of individual task constraints that will result in satisfying the overall process constraints. The architects must also sanity-check these constraints to determine whether they are practically achievable. Very often this sanity checking requires making task execution assignments, which is the topic of the next section.

Task Execution (`Performer`) and Management (`Requestor`) Assignments

After identifying the business process tasks and their corresponding performance constraints, the architects must then determine which participant will perform each of the tasks in the process. Part of this activity is determining that it is, indeed, feasible for that particular participant (whether human or system) to perform the task within the specified constraints. Arriving at a workable mix of task execution assignments and task constraints is a trial-and-error process. The number of possible combinations is yet another reason to think through the alternatives before any investment is made in implementing the business process.

When you assign task execution responsibility, you are assigning the role of `Performer` with respect to that task. You must also think about the role of `Requestor` with respect to that task. Specifically, you have to determine which of the task management communications (request, promise, results, and feedback) you will employ, determine which participants will handle each of these communications, and then determine which participants (if any) are in a position to determine whether the task completed successfully.

Let's look at the various work responsibility assignments that the architects are making in this activity. We'll begin with work assignments being made to people, and then examine the differences when systems are doing the work. Taking a simplified order delivery process, the architects might end up making the responsibility assignments shown in Figure 10–12. Here the `Warehouse Workgroup`'s receipt of the order serves the role of the *request* for the `Ship Orders` task. The `Shipped Goods` handoff to the `Delivery Service Workgroup` is similarly treated as the *request* for the `Deliver Orders` task.

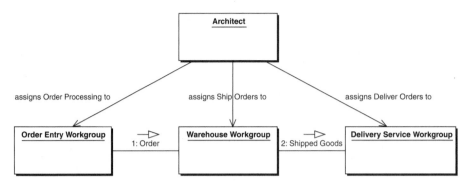

Figure 10–12: *Task Assignment in a Process*

The first thing to note here is that the architects are making work assignments. They are making decisions about what these work groups will be doing. But the architects are not in a position to commit those workgroups to actually do the work. This requires the concurrence of the workgroup itself.

The second thing to note is that none of the results are being sent back to the requestors. There is no feedback in the process as presently designed. Consequently, none of the participants is in a position to detect a failure in this process. You have a design without any task management. This type of design is highly prone to undetected breakdowns.

To remedy this situation, the business process architect can add to the process some notification communications, which announce the successful completion of the activity, as illustrated in Figure 10–13. Such extra communications do not add a great burden, but they add the ability to detect breakdowns in the process. In this example, the `Warehouse Workgroup` notifies the `Order Entry Workgroup` that the ordered goods have been shipped, and the `Delivery Service Workgroup` sends a notice when the goods have actually been delivered.

In order for breakdown detection to work, there is an additional responsibility assignment: The `Order Entry Workgroup` must look for this feedback and identify those orders that are overdue. They then must take corrective action. Once again, while the architects can make the assignments, only the `Order Entry Workgroup` can actually commit to doing the work.

Let's now look at the responsibility assignments when we are using systems in the individual workgroups to manage the work. Figure 10–14 shows the system-managed version of the original process. The architects

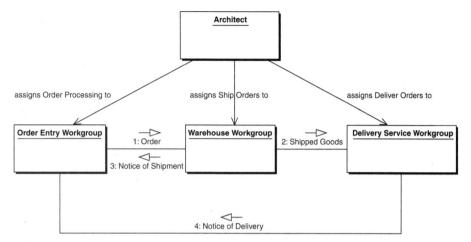

Figure 10–13: *Task Assignment Requiring Feedback*

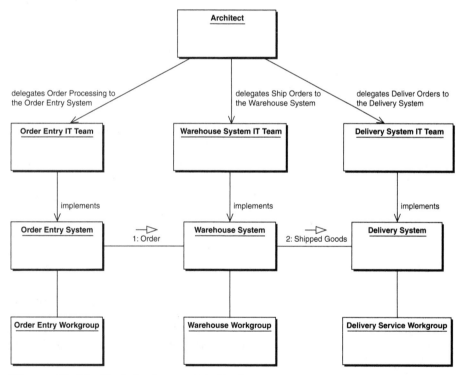

Figure 10–14: *Task Assignment to Systems*

are now making decisions about design-time responsibilities for the various IT teams, as well as the runtime responsibilities for both the systems and the workgroups. Once again, only the IT teams and workgroups can actually commit to fulfilling those responsibilities.

You can see that when tasks are delegated, the responsibility for the task management dialog must also be delegated. Just what this management dialog needs to be is itself a design decision, one that requires an understanding of both the overall business process and the system. Only the architects have this perspective.

Process Monitoring and Management

The actual management of the tasks at runtime is one of the responsibilities that the architects must identify and delegate. This involves more than simply receiving results or notifications. To be effective in actually managing these tasks, participants must be charged with determining whether the results actually arrived on time and with evaluating those results. These are specific monitoring and management responsibilities. If the `Order Entry Workgroup` in Figure 10–13 does not actively watch for the feedback and take action if orders are not shipped and delivered on time, you have accomplished little by providing the feedback.

The key responsibilities here are monitoring and management. The monitoring responsibility is to determine whether a breakdown has occurred and whether that breakdown is an outright failure to deliver a result or a less dramatic failure to meet service-level agreements. The management responsibility is to take corrective action when breakdowns occur, both with respect to the individual instance and as an overall process improvement. While the day-to-day operational responsibility is generally delegated, this management responsibility ultimately belongs to the business executive sponsor, who has responsibility for the overall business process. This is the person who actually owns the risks associated with the process not performing as planned.

The placement of these responsibilities has implications for the process and system design as well. If a single participant sends the initial request and has both monitoring and management responsibilities, providing the feedback to this participant is sufficient from a design perspective. But if these responsibilities are assigned to different participants, additional communications, and therefore additional design, are required. Thus, if the `Order Entry System` is responsible for monitoring the order, but the `Order Entry Workgroup` is responsible for managing the order, the system must communicate the existence of order breakdowns to the workgroup (Figure 10–15).

There are some subtleties in these work assignments. Strictly speaking, the `Order Entry System` cannot take responsibility for anything. Thus, it is actually the `Order Entry System IT Team` that is responsible for the system's monitoring of the process. This system also has no responsibility for managing the breakdowns, either. The `Order Entry Workgroup` has this responsibility.

These monitoring and management responsibility assignments are themselves task assignments. You have to concern yourself with the management of these tasks, just as you would with any other task. The

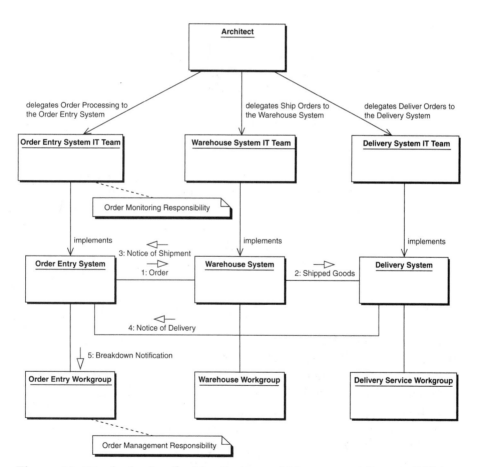

Figure 10–15: *Assigning the Monitoring and Management Responsibilities*

architects issued the requests, and they should be the ones to evaluate the results. But just what are these results? For tasks assigned to the IT teams, the results are test results that confirm the system's operation. In order for this to be effective, the systems architect must specify the required test results as part of the initial request. The IT executive sponsor plays a significant role here in ensuring the cooperation of the IT groups.

Since the systems cannot manage the breakdowns, the `Order Entry System` can only announce the existence of the breakdown to the `Order Entry Workgroup`. Once again, you need to obtain the actual commitment of this workgroup to manage these breakdowns. Only then will you have a robust business process. The business executive sponsor plays a critical role in ensuring the cooperation of the business groups.

Validating Results

Ensuring that a task generates a result is not enough to ensure that the overall process is successful. Producing erroneous results is just as bad as not producing results at all, maybe even worse. If you order a blender and receive a toaster, not only was your original request not fulfilled, but now you have the burden of having to return the toaster! In order to achieve a reliable process, it is prudent to evaluate the quality of results at various points in the process. Once again, the decisions as to which results should be validated and which participants should do the evaluation are design decisions. And once again, these design decisions are the responsibility of the business process and systems architects, and the authority to make the participants execute those responsibilities stems from the executive sponsors.

The Business Executive Sponsor Bears All Risks

Ultimately, the risks arising from the improper design and/or execution of the business process reside with the business executive sponsor. The sponsor can delegate the task of designing the process to the business process architect but retains the responsibility if the process design is a poor one. The sponsor can delegate the responsibility for the execution of the process to the participants but retains the responsibility if the process does not execute and provide the anticipated benefit.

It is in the executive sponsor's best interest to select skilled business process and systems architects and give them the support needed to do an effective job. Similarly, it is in the executive sponsor's best interest to incent the process participants to wholeheartedly support the process. Beyond this, the business executive sponsor must consider what type of information he or she needs to determine whether or not the process is executing properly. These information requirements define yet another set of task management communications that must be implemented in the business process.

A similar set of risks and responsibilities falls on the IT executive sponsor. This sponsor must measure and to encourage the various IT organizations involved in the design to wholeheartedly support the development, implementation, and operation of the system. The IT executive sponsor must consider what type of information he or she needs to verify whether or not the system is producing the required results and supporting the business process adequately. These information requirements define further task management communications that must be implemented within the system.

Summary

We create business processes and systems to perform and support specific types of work, and we depend on systems to perform some, if not all, of the tasks. But it cannot be said that systems are truly responsible for the tasks they perform. Such responsibility entails commitment: the ability to adapt to both expected and unexpected breakdowns in the performance of the tasks. Systems are fundamentally incapable of adapting to unexpected situations (at least in the present stage of evolution and into the foreseeable future). Indeed, systems can respond appropriately only to the situations they have been designed to handle. Thus, the true responsibility for these tasks lies with the people who design and support the systems. Only they can adapt to unexpected breakdowns in the work process.

In order for the design and support personnel to respond to an unexpected breakdown, they must first become aware that a breakdown has occurred. If a system is being used directly by a person and directly returns a result, that person is in a position to observe at least some of the unanticipated breakdowns and either handle them directly or communicate them to the appropriate design and support personnel. However, when one system directs another to perform work, there are no longer any people involved in the process to observe unexpected breakdowns. If you want a business process to gracefully handle the unexpected, you must build the systems to detect and report the unexpected.

Simply reporting an unexpected situation does not, by itself, result in an adaptive business process. The report must reach people, and these people must be committed to diagnosing the problem and taking corrective action. Traditionally, this responsibility has belonged to the design and support staff for the system components and has been perceived narrowly as a responsibility to maintain the system. The traditional response activities have focused on identifying the specific circumstance that the system was not designed to handle (or did not handle properly) and to fix it.

However, fixing the systems component does not salvage the business work that was in progress when the error occurred. You may need to involve people in order to recover this work. Furthermore, these people may be in an entirely different organization than the one maintaining the system itself. They will need to be notified of the work interruption and must be organized to respond accordingly. Different information may be required in this notification to identify the unit of work that was affected. Since the state of this work may be distributed across a number of systems, recovery actions may require interaction with multiple systems.

All of these human interactions have design implications for both the business processes and the systems. The systems must be designed to recognize unexpected situations and notify the appropriate people. The business process by which these people respond must be designed. Any system interfaces required to support the investigation of the problem and the subsequent recovery actions must be added.

If these design implications are recognized and considered early in the design cycle, you can ensure that the points of breakdown detection are clearly defined. You can implement a uniform breakdown annunciation scheme and a managed response. Adding the required promise or result communication to a design, or adding a result evaluation, can generally be accommodated with a modest effort as long as these ideas are part of the initial design process. However, retrofitting such capabilities on an existing implementation can be very expensive, particularly if the communications required for breakdown detection are not already a part of the system design.

Key Process Design Questions

1. Looking at the overall business process, how can breakdowns in the process be detected? Have elements of the task management dialog been omitted? If so, what are the implications for the business process?

2. Where responses are expected, have service-level agreements been defined that establish the allowed time frame for receiving the responses? Do the responses include status information from the responding party?

3. Are all results being evaluated to determine whether or not they are correct? If not, what will the symptoms be and what will the downstream consequences be?

4. Have all of the process responsibilities been explicitly assigned? Who is responsible for:

   a. Designing the basic process flow?

   b. Establishing the task performance constraints?

   c. Assigning task execution responsibilities?

   d. Assigning process monitoring and management responsibilities?

   e. Assigning results validation responsibilities?

Suggested Reading

Rumbaugh, James, Ivar Jacobson, and Grady Booch. 2005. *The Unified Modeling Language Reference Manual, Second Edition.* Boston, MA: Addison-Wesley.

Solomon, Robert C., and Fernando Flores. 2001. *Building Trust: In Business, Politics, Relationships, and Life.* New York: Oxford University Press.

Winograd, Terry, and Fernando Flores. 1986. *Understanding Computers and Cognition: A New Foundation for Design.* Reading, MA: Addison-Wesley.

Chapter 11

Managing Project Risk

When you can measure what you are speaking about, and express it in numbers, you know something about it; but when you cannot measure it, when you cannot express it in numbers, your knowledge is of a meager and unsatisfactory kind: it may be the beginning of knowledge, but you have scarcely, in your thoughts, advanced to the stage of science.

—William Thomson, Lord Kelvin,
Popular Lectures and Addresses (1891–1894)

Errors using inadequate data are much less than those using no data at all.

—Charles Babbage (1792–1871)

A project, at least in the context of this book, is a coordinated effort to alter the business process and systems fabric of an enterprise in order to realize specific benefits. We are all familiar with how such projects get started: Somebody concludes that achieving certain benefits warrants an investment in altering this fabric. The idea is shopped around for a while, and eventually a decision is made to proceed with a project. Budget is allocated, a project team is assembled and chartered, and the project is under way.

Sadly, many of these projects are not successful. By some measures, up to 30% of IT projects are never completed, and up to 70% never deliver the expected benefits.[1] How can this happen? With so much at stake and so much being invested, how can projects have such high failure rates? While more has been written on this subject than I have space to accommodate here, an examination of this literature reveals that the root causes of these project failures are the very same issues discussed in Chapter 10: responsibility, communication, trust, and commitment—all related to achieving the project goals.

Many, if not all, of these problems can be avoided by getting a project off on the right track with well-defined objectives and a sound governance process. This is the intent of the project charter. The charter establishes measurable goals, defines the constraints on the project, identifies the individuals playing leadership roles, and defines the governance process that will be used to manage the project. The governance process is crucial. It ensures that there is an ongoing, open, and frank dialog between the oversight team and the project team. This dialog allows the oversight team, and most importantly the business executive sponsor, to respond appropriately to problems. The timeliness of this communication and response is particularly important when project goals turn out to be more difficult to achieve than initially anticipated.

The Project as a Dialog

To help you understand what needs to be in the project charter, I'll examine an entire project as if it were a single conversation for action, as discussed in Chapter 10. This conversation, consisting of a request, promise, result, and feedback, is a dialog between the business executive sponsor and the project team. The task is to realize specific benefits for the enterprise. What exactly needs to be in each of these communications between the executive sponsor and the project team in order for the project to be successful? To make this discussion more concrete, consider a retail bank that wishes to reduce the cost of providing its services by adding an ATM service.

---

1. Robert Frese and Vicki Sauter, "Project Success and Failure: What Is Success, What Is Failure, and How Can You Improve Your Odds for Success?" (2003).

What is the actual request? What exactly is the project team being asked to do? Is it to purchase, program, and deploy an ATM network? Well, that may be one of the things the project team ends up doing, but that is not the purpose of the project. The purpose of the project is to reduce the per-transaction operating cost for the bank from its current $3 per transaction to less than $1 per transaction.

Phrasing the request this way immediately clarifies the scope of the project. The task is not only to design and install an ATM network but also to do so in a way that makes possible an overall operating cost of $1 per transaction. Thus, the project team needs to consider the cost of installing and maintaining ATM machines and the cost of issuing ATM cards, as well as the actual creation of the ATM network. What else needs to be included in the request? How about the expectations concerning how long the team has to get the job done and the expected level of investment?

What is the expected project result? Nothing less than an operational business process that executes customer banking transactions at a cost of $1 per transaction. This implies that the ATM system has to first be deployed, and then the operating costs need to be measured in order to establish that the goal has been reached. Data must be collected about the transaction volume, initial investments, and ongoing operational expenses. This data must be analyzed and projected into the future in order to determine whether the per-transaction costs will reach the intended target. The real project results are these measurements!

In this project-as-a-dialog, the final feedback to the project team is the business executive sponsor's evaluation of the project's expenditures and the ongoing operational costs. This feedback indicates to the project team whether an acceptable level of benefit has been reached or whether more resources need to be applied to achieve a further operational cost reduction.

The one element of the dialog not mentioned thus far is the promise. This is largely (and unfortunately) because in the typical conduct of a project, there isn't one. Projects are typically chartered with a vaguely defined scope and budgetary guesstimates as to the required level of time and effort. There is an implied assumption that the project's goals can actually be achieved within these cost and schedule guidelines—an assumption that is often in error.

The solution to this problem is to introduce an explicit promise into the dialog between the oversight team and the project team. This promise represents a commitment on the part of the project team—the development personnel and the operations personnel—to deliver the expected benefit within the cost and schedule guidelines. In the ATM example, the development personnel commit to delivering the ATM business processes and systems within the development budget, and the operations personnel commit to achieving a per-transaction operating expense of less than $1. The work leading up to this commitment—this promise—focuses primarily on defining the scope and answering the feasibility question.

In order for this promise to work, the business executive sponsor must be willing and prepared to accept feedback that it is not possible to achieve the expected benefits within the given constraints. The governance process must also allow for a subsequent dialog between the oversight team and the project team as alternatives of benefits, scope, and budget are explored. The outcome of this subsequent dialog may be an updated charter for the project—or the termination of the project. But either way, it must be recognized that the best interests of the enterprise are being served.

The Project Charter

Let's back up now with this project-as-a-dialog perspective in mind and look at what needs to be in the project charter. One element is, of course, the request—an explicit statement of what the project team is being asked to do. A second element is a clear identification of who the participants are in the dialog—the oversight team and the project team. The third and final element is a description of the governance process—the required dialog between the oversight team and the project team over the course of the project. These three elements comprise the project charter.

The Request

The request being made of the project team is to reach a particular business goal. Clearly stating that goal is essential to getting the project headed in the right direction from the very beginning. Making such a clear statement requires covering at least three topics: the expected benefits, the constraints under which the benefits are to be achieved, and the risks that will accrue to the enterprise should the benefits not be achieved. In order for the project team to do its job properly and efficiently, it must have a clear understanding of each of these topics.

Expected Benefits

Every project is expected to deliver some form of benefit to the enterprise—after all, that's the purpose of the project! But a vague statement of the expected benefit will not lead to success, at least not efficiently. Consequently, the charter of the ATM project does not just talk generically about lowering the per-transaction cost of doing business; it sets specific goals such as lowering the per-transaction cost to $1 and having 50% of the bank's transactions performed through the ATM machine. Such quantification of expected benefits is absolutely essential. It allows design alternatives to be evaluated in terms of their relative ability to provide these benefits and provides objective criteria for determining the overall success or failure of the project.

As the quotation from Lord Kelvin at the beginning of this chapter reminds us, if you cannot put numbers on something, your understanding of it is necessarily vague. Vagueness, in turn, makes it difficult to communicate. In a project setting, vagueness in stating the expected project benefits makes it difficult for the oversight team to clearly communicate what is expected of the project team and for the project team to evaluate its own progress. Vagueness makes achieving success a subjective judgment, and you can't afford such vagueness in your projects—there is too much at stake.

This is not to imply that quantification is easy. However, the time spent determining an appropriate quantification is time well spent. A project's goal might be to improve customer satisfaction, but how exactly is this customer satisfaction to be measured? By survey? In terms of repeat customers? By a lower rate of returns on orders? Real thought is required on the part of the oversight team to transform vague goals into concrete, measurable objectives. This effort is worthwhile. The act of making the goal quantifiable will actually help the business executive sponsor to clarify project expectations. Such clarification is essential to success, for if the sponsor is unable to clearly state the actual goal, how on earth is the project team expected to determine what it will take to achieve that goal? For that matter, if the goal is not quantified, how can you be assured that the project team's perception of the goal is at all consistent with the sponsor's real intent?

The conclusion then is that the project charter must clearly state the specific measurable benefits expected from the project. It must also specify the measurements that must be made to determine whether these benefits have been realized. In reality, it is only when these benefits have been measurably achieved that the project can be deemed successful.

Constraints

Hand in hand with project benefits go the constraints under which these benefits must be achieved. The most common constraints are the cost and schedule guidelines for the project. You initiate projects when you conclude that achieving certain benefits warrants making a specific level of investment, provided those benefits can be obtained within a specific time frame. Both the level of investment and the corresponding time frame are essential elements of this decision. Both must be made clear to the project team so that it can not only remain within these bounds but also make a determination as to whether it is even possible to achieve the expected benefits within these bounds. For example, the ATM project might have a two-year time horizon and a budget of $10 million for getting 50% of the bank's transactions performed via ATM machines at an operational cost of $1 per transaction.

There are often other constraints on a project as well, and the nature of these constraints tends to vary greatly from project to project. Such constraints might indicate specific technologies that should (or should not) be employed, specific applications and systems that should (or should not) be used, or specific standards and best practices that must be adhered to. In the ATM project, for example, there might be a constraint that all of the ATM machines must be physically located at existing bank branch offices.

Documenting these additional constraints in the project charter lowers the project's cost and risk. If these constraints are not specified at the beginning of the project, the project team is left to discover them as it encounters the stakeholders who will impose the constraints. Such ad hoc discovery can be costly, as the constraints may not be discovered until after design commitments have been made or implementation actually begun. The resulting rework and delays will play havoc with the project cost and schedule and may push the project beyond the committed cost and schedule limits. For this reason, it is always best to explicitly specify these constraints in the project charter. The ATM project, for example, might require adherence to specific regulatory and internal bank security requirements. To the extent that these requirements are already known, referencing them in the project charter can only make the project go more smoothly.

Project Risks and Rewards

Part of understanding the project's goal lies in knowing what will happen to the enterprise if the goal is not reached—if the quantified benefits are not actually achieved within the given constraints. This is important because the project team is continually making design decisions that trade off different levels of investment against different levels of benefit achievement. In order to make wise investment decisions, the team needs to understand what will happen if the benefits are under- or overachieved or if the constraints are almost but not quite satisfied.

As an example, consider an online retailer that is losing its competitive position in the marketplace due to cost pressures. The business executive sponsor concludes that the company needs to reduce its cost of sales. The chartered purpose of the project (i.e., the expected benefit) is to reduce the average labor cost associated with a sale (including the handling of returns) by 25%. But what would happen to the enterprise if the actual improvement is only 23%? Or on the positive side, what would happen if a modest additional investment (but beyond the project charter) could reduce the labor cost by 28%?

Understanding these consequences provides guidance for the project team as it makes design and investment decisions. In the retail example, it is important for the project team to know that an improvement of at least 15% is necessary to keep the enterprise profitable and that an improvement of 25% is needed to meet stockholder's expectations concerning corporate profitability. Furthermore, any improvement beyond 25% will go directly into increased profits. Therefore, improvements beyond 25% are desirable, provided that the required additional investment is modest. Understanding this landscape puts the project team in a far better position to make good business decisions and to recommend appropriate variations in the planned investment, particularly during the negotiations leading up to the promise.

Other projects may have very different types of risks associated with them. Projects oriented toward compliance with regulatory requirements or service-level agreements may have very sharp risk thresholds, particularly when financial penalties are involved. Exceeding the threshold will trigger the penalty clause and result in an immediate cost to the enterprise. For example, in the United States there is a regulation for financial institutions that imposes a fine of $10,000 per incident if a customer has told the institution not to contact him or her and the institution does so anyway. It does the enterprise no good to almost succeed in its efforts to avoid calling the customer (perhaps due to a bug); a miss is as good as a mile. The project team needs to understand that there is no leeway—it either achieves the objective (with a high level of probability) or it has wasted the project's investment.

The more that the project team understands about the business situation and the associated business risks and rewards, the better able it will be to do its job. The banking project will correctly conclude that while a Rube Goldberg[2] approach to communicating customer do-not-call information between a financial institution's systems might be the least expensive to implement, the resulting unreliable systems present an unacceptable risk to the enterprise. The retail project will be on the lookout for design alternatives that might increase productivity beyond the target 25%. With such understanding, projects will become focused on the real needs of the enterprise.

Key Participants

In order for the project to be successful, the project charter must clearly establish the lines of authority for the project. The business executive sponsor must be clearly identified so that everyone knows who is chartering the project. This is the only person who can change the scope and constraints for the project and resolve conflicts between the project team's priorities and the business silo priorities. Similarly, the IT executive sponsor must be clearly identified so that everyone knows who will resolve conflicts between the project's priorities and the priorities of the various IT groups.

If there is an oversight team for the project, the charter should indicate the makeup of that oversight team and the reporting relationships between the project, the oversight team, and the business executive sponsor. For small projects, this might be the manager of the enterprise

---

2. Rube Goldberg (1883–1970) was a cartoonist famous for drawing exceedingly and unnecessarily complicated mechanisms for performing trivial tasks.

projects group discussed in Chapter 6. For larger initiatives, a specially constituted oversight committee may be formulated to guide the effort. In any case, the charter should clearly indicate the limits of the oversight team's authority when the business executive sponsor is not directly involved.

Finally, the project charter must indicate who is playing each of the three project leadership roles: the project manager, the business process architect, and the systems architect. Since no real work can occur without these people, they need to be identified before the project even begins.

Project Governance

Project governance is essentially the formalization of the dialog between the oversight team and the project team. The project charter should clearly define this governance process, explicitly delineating the required minimum dialog between the two teams. The charter should indicate what form these interactions will take (usually a written report and a summary presentation) and the time frame within which each interaction is expected to occur. If these governance practices are well documented, the charter can simply reference this documentation. Otherwise, the charter needs to spell out the governance process that will be used.

For best results, there should be a bare minimum of five interactions between the two teams:

1. The chartering of the project
2. The commitment (or negative feasibility assessment)
3. The development approval
4. The benefit measurement
5. The feedback regarding the benefit measurements

These interactions represent the major milestones in the project's progress (Figure 11–1). For lengthy projects, it is entirely appropriate to introduce other intermediate milestones to track progress between these major milestones.

The first of these interaction milestones is the *chartering of the project*. The charter, whose content was outlined earlier, constitutes a formal request from the oversight team to the project team to do whatever work is necessary to produce the expected benefits for the enterprise.

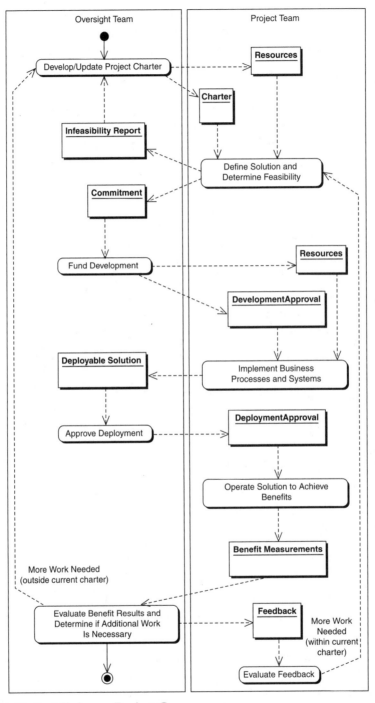

Figure 11–1: *Minimum Project Governance*

This milestone marks the formal chartering of the project team and must be accompanied by a budget and resource allocation sufficient to reach the next project milestone, the commitment.

The second milestone, assuming that the project team concludes that the project is feasible within the cost and schedule guidelines, is the *commitment*. The commitment constitutes a promise on the part of the project team to actually generate the specified benefits within the cost and schedule guidelines. The oversight team accepts this commitment by providing the resources required to execute the remainder of the project.

On the other hand, the project team might conclude that the project is not feasible. This report is delivered to the oversight team and ultimately to the business executive sponsor. The sponsor will then decide whether to alter the project charter (based on this report) or cancel the project. *For this communication to be frank and honest, it must be made very clear to the project team that there is no stigma associated with reporting the project as infeasible and that such feedback is highly desirable as early in the project as possible.*

The third milestone, the *deployment approval*, marks the readiness to deploy the changes to the enterprise's business process and system fabric and the oversight team's approval to proceed. Up to this point, there has been no actual alteration of the day-to-day operations of the enterprise. The oversight team makes the final decision as to whether these changes should actually be deployed.

The fourth milestone is the *benefit measurement*. Once the deployment has been approved and the changes put into place, data must be collected to measure the actual benefit that has been realized. While the governance process in the diagram shows the delivery of this measurement information as a single interaction with the oversight team, more likely it will take the form of periodic reporting, with each report being evaluated by the oversight team. Based on this evaluation, the management team may direct the project team to make further changes within the scope of the current project charter or may decide to alter the project charter and begin another dialog.

The fifth and final milestone is the *feedback regarding the benefit measurements*. This milestone marks the oversight team's acknowledgment that the desired benefit has been realized and marks the formal conclusion of the project.

The dialog described here is a representative example of a governance dialog but will need to be tailored to the specifics and culture of the actual organization. While variations are to be expected, it is important to clearly define and document the actual planned governance dialog in the project charter. Such clarity is required to set expectations and avoid miscommunication between the project and oversight teams.

The Project Exit Strategy

The period between the deployment of the business processes and systems and the conclusion of the project is an awkward time in the lifecycle of a project. During this time, the oversight team is receiving benefit measurements and trying to determine whether the project has successfully achieved its goals. The awkwardness comes in deciding how much of the development team to leave in place. From a pure cost perspective, the oversight team would like to disband the development team. But if the development team is completely disbanded, who will make needed alterations if the benefits are not being achieved as desired?

What is commonly done is to retain a substantial part of the full team in the time period immediately following the initial go-live and then gradually ramp down the staffing level as confidence in the stability of the business processes and systems grows and their ability to produce the desired benefits solidifies. Long before this point, however, assumptions about rampdown have been made for budgetary and planning purposes. These assumptions are effectively part of the cost and schedule constraints and thus should be documented in the project charter. These assumptions need to be validated and adjusted at each of the project milestones.

Considerations in Structuring Projects

The discussion so far treats projects as if each one has a single release. However, for larger projects, a single "big bang" release is a high-risk proposition. Such projects are often partitioned into multiple phases and sometimes even multiple projects.

Phased Projects and Services Development

When a project is implemented as a series of releases, there are often dependencies between later releases and earlier releases. Later releases typically build on services implemented in earlier releases, incorporating this earlier functionality into additional business processes. Such services obviously must be designed with the later usage in mind, or else inefficient rework will be required to enhance the service to support the new utilization.

Designing services for future usage does not happen by accident. Architectural work must look ahead to future releases when designing the business processes and systems. This, in turn, has implications for requirements gathering, as the requirements for these future uses must be understood before the service can be appropriately designed. Thus the project must be organized so that the business process and systems architects are designing with these future needs in mind, even though the early deployments may contain only a subset of the design.

Partitioned Projects

When the business and IT worlds are highly siloed, it is not at all unusual to have separate development teams in the separate silos, each focused on a different set of systems. Unfortunately, it is all too common for such work to be totally partitioned into separate projects with no common oversight and design effort. These separate projects end up with separate charters, separate management teams, and separate design teams. Partitioning of this type completely loses sight of the real overall business objective. Nobody is charged with achieving that objective. This becomes apparent when you try to state the business benefit expected of the individual projects because there isn't one! The individual projects, on their own, provide no business benefit whatsoever. It is only when all of the projects are successfully completed that any business benefit can be realized.

Completely partitioning the project into separate projects loses the focus on the overall business benefit. No longer is there anyone asking what changes are required to the business processes and systems to achieve the expected benefit. No longer is there a unified view of the overall business process or the overall system architecture. You are back in the situation depicted earlier in Figure 6–2, with nobody in charge. There is no business executive sponsor to ensure cooperation and focus on attaining the overall business benefit. There are no business process and systems architects focused on ensuring that the fragments of business processes and systems fit together into a coherent whole. There is nobody accountable for producing the real business benefit.

Such project structures are to be assiduously avoided. While it may be entirely appropriate to have distinct development teams working on different portions of the business processes and systems, in order to ensure a successful outcome, the workings of these teams and the overall design of the system must be centrally coordinated. This central coordination must include the full spectrum of involved operations personnel as well. To achieve the overall business goals, the five key roles outlined previously must be staffed and chartered with the overall responsibility for the combined projects. These leadership responsibilities must therefore span all of the development and operational teams involved. Without this central focus, achieving the desired business benefit is unlikely.

Cosmic Chicken

Remember the project prime objective? It is to determine whether the desired benefits are achievable within the cost and schedule guidelines and to realize those benefits if they are. Implicit in this directive is a requirement to inform the business executive sponsor as soon as possible if the goals do not appear achievable within these cost and schedule guidelines. Of course, the sponsor must be open to this possibility and receptive to the communication of this bad news. A lack of openness leads to the hiding of the truth until such time as it can no longer be hidden.

Sometimes this lack of openness, coupled with the partitioning of a project into multiple projects, spawns a risky political game—one that has been referred to as a cosmic game of chicken. In this game, each project has its own team and its own goals. None of the teams actually believes that its goals are achievable within the cost and schedule guidelines, but none of the teams wants to be the bearer of bad tidings. As the game progresses, each of the teams moves forward, doing work and expending resources, each hoping that one of the others will be the first one forced to admit that its goals cannot be met. The crash at the end is inevitable. The only question is who will chicken out first.

Such games are, of course, bad for the enterprise as a whole. Furthermore, they are totally avoidable. The circumstances leading to the game involve fragmenting what ought to be a single project into multiple projects without providing any overall management and common design. Avoiding such situations requires that the five roles we have been discussing be actively played. The business executive sponsor must actively manage the overall effort, with the IT executive sponsor aligning the IT resources. There must be an overall project manager, a business process architect, and a systems architect to determine what the overall solution should look like and to coordinate the work in the individual silos. Finally, there must be a commitment: an explicit determination of project feasibility actively supported by all participants. The alternative is the expensive game of cosmic chicken.

Summary

The project charter is the first milestone in the path toward a successful project. It frames the project in a concise manner, presenting the goals of the project, the major players on both the oversight and project teams, and the governance process that will be used to manage the project. The charter is the formal request to the project team from the oversight team. Its purpose is to clearly state what the project team is being asked to do, the constraints under which the team is being asked to do it, and the risks associated with failing to meet the objectives.

The manner in which this information is presented is far less important than simply making a conscientious effort to document this information and establish a working governance process. The advantage provided by the project charter lies in clearly stating the problem to be solved. The charter clarifies the goals by quantifying the expected benefits, making the constraints clear, and spelling out the risks. It defines who is responsible for producing the benefits by identifying the leadership of the oversight and project teams. Its specification of the governance process defines the expected dialog between the two teams during the course of producing these results.

Finally, I should emphasize once again the importance of the commitment in the governance dialog. The constraints specified in the project charter represent the business executive sponsor's statement that this particular level of investment is warranted by the expected benefits. Determining whether or not the benefits can actually be achieved within those constraints is an important first step in the project. This step also requires that the oversight team be prepared to accept and respond to a negative answer. This dialog between the two teams gives the oversight team the opportunity to reset expectations and adjust its investment strategy with a minimal initial investment in time and resources.

Key Project Risk Management Questions

1. Has a project charter been written that quantifies the expected benefits, defines the constraints under which these benefits must be achieved, and spells out the risks of not achieving those benefits?

2. Does the project charter define the oversight team and the leadership of the project team? Are the business executive sponsor, IT executive sponsor, project manager, business process architect, and systems architect named, available, and committed to their roles?

3. Is the governance process for the project defined? Does it include an explicit commitment step and allow for a finding that the benefits cannot be achieved within the specified constraints?

4. Has a tentative transition plan for concluding the project been defined?

5. Will the project result in a single release, or are there multiple phases to the project? If there are multiple phases, how is the scope of each phase to be determined, and how will the multiple phases be coordinated?

6. Is the project really a portion of a larger effort? If so, is there appropriate governance in place over the larger effort?

Suggested Reading

Frese, Robert, and Vicki Sauter. 2003. "Project Success and Failure: What Is Success, What Is Failure, and How Can You Improve Your Odds for Success?" St. Louis, MO: University of Missouri–St. Louis. www.umsl.edu/~sauter/analysis/6840_f03_papers/frese/.

Chapter 12

Investing Wisely in Risk Reduction

We turn now to consider what kind of investment is appropriate in trying to reduce risks. Specifically, to what extent should you let the consideration of risk alter the design of the business process and the supporting systems?

First, you need an understanding of what the risks actually are, and you need to understand the extent to which each potential business process or system design change will actually reduce the risk. You also need to express that change in risk in such a way that you can then meaningfully weigh it against the potential investment, reaching a reasonable conclusion as to whether that particular investment is worthwhile. Finally, you want to perform this comparison in a way that you can record and then share the rationale behind the decision.

This discussion of risk must begin with two frank admissions of reality. The first is that regardless of the level of investment you make, risks can never be completely eliminated. There is no zero-risk approach to doing anything. Even if you keep redundant copies of business records in several places, it is still possible to destroy all copies. Even if you have redundant systems in several locations, it is still possible for all of these systems to fail at the same time. So you need to understand the level of risk that the enterprise can tolerate.

The second admission of reality is that risk reduction requires investment. Establishing any given level of risk requires a corresponding level of investment. Since the resources you have to invest are finite, you can't establish a given level of risk as being acceptable without considering first whether that level is even attainable with the resources available.

So risk management boils down to trading off the level of risk against the corresponding investment required to attain that level of risk. It requires reaching a reasonable compromise. Furthermore, while the techniques for risk reduction may involve investments in business process design and technology, determining the appropriate tradeoff between risk and investment is fundamentally a business decision. The business executive sponsor is the person who ultimately makes the investment and bears the resulting risk. The project team makes decisions on behalf of this sponsor and so must engage the sponsor and business units to understand the business impact of process failures.

The Risk of Failure

When thinking of risks, the first type that comes to mind is that of outright failure—a failure of the process to produce the expected results when they are needed. For example, when you step on the brake pedal in your car, you expect the car to stop—now! If the brakes fail to operate at the time you step on the brake pedal, you have a serious problem. In this example, you can see two dimensions of failure: One is whether or not the expected result is produced, and the other is whether or not that result is produced when it is needed. Stepping on the brake pedal and having the brakes engage a minute later is just as bad as the brakes not working at all.

You will find time-critical processes in businesses as well. When a stock market trade order is placed, the timeliness of the order execution is as important as the trade itself. The decision to trade is based on current market conditions, and delaying the execution can result in the trade occurring under significantly different conditions. Such delays can produce results that are very different from those expected.

With business processes, there are a number of different ways in which a process might fail. It might simply be unavailable when it is needed because somebody didn't show up for work or because a system is down. Work in progress in the process might get lost because the folder containing the work was misplaced or a disk containing the information crashed. An error in the business logic may result in a failure to produce the desired result.

Each type of failure tends to impact the business in slightly different ways. Some of these failures (e.g., losing the folder) impact just a single unit of work, while others impact many. Each type of failure typically requires a different mitigation strategy as well. This variability makes it necessary to understand both the types of failures that can occur and the cost impacts of each type before you can make any decisions about which types of investments to make in mitigation strategies.

While each business process is different, as is each system architecture, some of the typical types of failures can be illustrated and analyzed with a few examples. Consider the four different businesses profiled in Table 12–1. Three of these businesses (A, B, and C) are similar in nature because each is engaged in selling goods through a web site. These three differ primarily in the size of the business. The fourth business is an extreme contrast, a construction business doing large jobs. Whereas the sales businesses have a high volume of individually low-value jobs (considering each order as a job), the construction business has a very small number of very high-value jobs.

Let's look at some of the failure risks these businesses face and weigh those risks against some of the investments the businesses might make

Table 12–1: *Profile of Four Businesses*

	Business A	Business B	Business C	Business D
Annual sales	$1,000,000	$10,000,000	$100,000,000	$100,000,000
Average order value	$20	$50	$250	$33,000,000
Average orders/day	137	548	1,096	<1
Peak orders/ hour	17	68	137	<1
Average order fulfillment cycle (days)	3	3	3	365

in mitigating them. Bear in mind, the intent here is not to explore the breadth of available risk mitigation strategies (I will do that in the companion volume, *SOA in Practice: Implementing Total Architecture*), nor is the intent to show techniques for investment analysis. The purpose is twofold: (1) to illustrate that exploring risk mitigation strategies and investment opportunities is senseless without an understanding of the business consequences of failures and (2) to indicate the type of understanding you need.

Loss of Resources

The first failure to consider is the loss of a resource needed to operate the business process. This might be the consequence of a machine being down or someone being out sick. Such failures result in the overall business process not being available for some period of time. For systems, this interval is the time it takes to realize that the system is down and to diagnose and repair the system. For personnel, this interval is the time it takes to realize that someone is missing (or not doing his or her job) and to either find replacement personnel or get the missing person back onto the assigned task.

Such occurrences are certainly not unusual: The complexities of organizations, machines, networks, operating systems, databases, and applications combined with interruptions of infrastructure services such as telephone, power, and air conditioning make such disruptions inevitable. So what should we invest in reducing these outages? Should we have extra personnel on standby to fill in? Should we have spare machines ready to go? Let's look at the costs of these failures and some common mitigation strategies to see what might be appropriate.

One mitigation strategy for systems is to invest in extra machines with the intent of reducing service outage times. When all factors are considered, an ordinary low-end server with no special power conditioning, air conditioning, or other protections might have an availability of 99%. If the server is supposed to be up continuously around the clock, a 99% availability would result in approximately 88 hours of downtime a year. Typically, such a system will go down a number of times during the year, each time requiring the better part of the day to diagnose and fix the problems.

If you assume that the consequence of the system being down is that the business loses to a competitor the orders that would have been received during that time, you can estimate the worst-case annual losses by multiplying the peak order rate by the average value of each order and the total duration of the outages. This approach characterizes an online order business quite well, giving the estimated revenue losses shown in Table 12–2. Such outages could be expected to result in up to $10,000 annual lost revenue for Business A, $100,000 for Business B, and $1,000,000 for Business C.

What kind of risk mitigation investment might be warranted in these cases? If the availability of the system were increased to 99.9%, Business A could be expected to avoid the loss of $9,000 in revenue, Business B could avoid $90,000, and Business C could avoid $900,000. These numbers present very different investment options for these businesses.

Based on this admittedly crude analysis, Business A might be able to justify a single investment such as the purchase of a backup server or an uninterruptible power supply. Such small savings justify modest investments at best, but such modest investments are only enough to take a stab at the problem. It is unlikely that a $9,000 investment would allow the business to actually achieve a tenfold improvement in system availability. Business B, on the other hand, can justify a number of investments including backup machines, uninterruptible power supplies, alternate network connections, and the like. Business C not only has sufficient justification for a comprehensive program of availability improvement, it even has justification for moving on to fault tolerance techniques that might help it approach 99.99% availability. Even though these businesses are similar in nature, their differences in sales volume yield very different investment strategies for risk mitigation.

But what does a loss of system availability do to our construction business? System outages in this business will result not in a loss of orders but rather in a degradation of productivity for people working in the

Table 12–2: *Impact of System Outages on Online Sales Businesses*

System Availability (Single-Shift Operation, 7 Days/Week)	Annual Lost Time (Hours)	Annual Lost Revenue (Approximate)		
		Business A	Business B	Business C
99%	29.2	$10,000	$100,000	$1,000,000
99.9%	2.92	$1,000	$10,000	$100,000
99.99%	0.292	$100	$1,000	$10,000

business. If you assume that half the revenue of the business is for salaries (the other half for materials used in construction), the business spends about $50 million annually on salaries. If people spend on average 25% of their time using the system (for drafting, project management, materials ordering, and so on), 25% of the annual salary expenditure would be impacted by system downtime—a maximum of $12.5 million. Assuming that productivity deteriorates proportionally to the loss of system availability, you get the productivity losses shown in Table 12–3.

You can see from this analysis that increasing system availability from 99% to 99.9% will result in an annual savings of $112,500—a significant number to be sure, but nearly an order of magnitude less than Business C with the same total revenue. Clearly, you need to understand the nature of the business in order to understand the appropriate level of investment in reducing system outages. Similar thinking would go into the design of the business process and the availability of personnel. If a pilot calls in sick, the plane will not fly unless a replacement is found. Airlines make considerable investments in having backup personnel readily available to ensure that flights stick to their schedules.

Loss of Data

Another potential failure to be taken seriously is the loss of data. The loss of work-in-progress records, whether in paper or electronic form, will result in a failure to produce the desired results. Table 12–4 shows the impact on the online order businesses resulting from a loss of all the orders in the pipeline. Once again, you see that Business A could justify a modest investment that might include purchasing a tape backup system and making nightly copies of the data. This would reduce the risk to the loss of a single day's orders. Business B, on the

Table 12–3: *Impact of System Outages on a Construction Business*

System Availability (Single-Shift Operation, 5 Days/Week)	Annual Lost Time (Hours)	Annual Productivity Losses, Business D
99%	5.125	$125,000
99.9%	0.5125	$12,500
99.99%	0.05125	$1,250

Table 12–4: *Impact of Data Loss on Online Order Businesses*

	Business A	Business B	Business C
Number of orders in pipeline	411	1,644	3,288
Potential revenue loss (value of orders in pipeline)	$8,220	$82,200	$822,000

other hand, could justify the use of a fault-tolerant RAID (redundant array of independent disks) subsystem for its disk storage and thus avoid any loss of orders in the event of a single disk failure. Based on this data, Business C might be able to justify the cost of a second data center and the active replication of data between them so that even in the event of the loss of an entire data center, no orders would be lost.

Determining the impact on the construction business is, once again, a bit different. The time people spend working with systems in this business is time spent developing and executing construction plans. The plans are saved in the systems, and a loss of the system would require the re-creation of the plans, a time-consuming exercise. Using the numbers provided earlier, if you assume that half of the business revenue is for labor, and 25% of that time is spent maintaining information in the systems, then there is $12,500,000 invested in the information stored in the systems. Obviously not all of this would have to be re-created in the event of a disk failure, but certainly a substantial portion would, not to mention the cost of the delay to the project itself. Given the nature of the business, a daily backup of information would limit the risk to the loss of $32,000 worth of work. This could be further reduced to virtually zero through the use of a RAID storage subsystem, which might warrant an investment in one.

Logic Failure

Processes are not perfect. Logic errors, whether human or machine, can also result in the process not producing the required results. The increasing complexity of software, the frequency with which business rules are changed and features added, and the pressure to deploy these changes rapidly all limit the amount of time that can be devoted to software testing. People-oriented processes are rarely tested before they are used in production. These situations tend to increase the number of undiscovered logic errors in the business process—errors that can result in the system not generating the desired results. These errors then impact a percentage of the work flowing through the system. The risk is that the error will go undetected and uncorrected and result in a loss of revenue.

Various strategies can be employed to reduce this risk. One is to increase the amount of predeployment testing and thus reduce the percentage of the work impacted. This will immediately provide a statistical reduction in the number of affected jobs. A second strategy is continuous process improvement, that is, monitoring the flow of work, identifying problems in the process, and correcting those problems so that future work will be handled properly. Over time, this also will provide a statistical reduction in the number of affected jobs. A third strategy is to monitor, detect, and correct problems in each job as they occur. This will reduce the likelihood that any given job will fail to produce the expected result. Each of these strategies, however, requires a different kind of investment. So the key question is this: What level of investment in which of these strategies is warranted?

If we assume that a logic error impacts one out of every hundred orders and the result is a loss of revenue from the affected orders, the revenue loss will range from $10,000 for Business A to $1,000,000 for Business C (Table 12–5). A tenfold reduction in this error rate would result in a range of savings from $9,000 for business A to $900,000 for Business C. A potential revenue improvement of $9,000 might help Business A to justify the development of some management reports aimed at identifying errors and root causes (a very limited attempt at continuous process improvement), but not much more. With a potential $90,000 bottom-line improvement, Business B might be able to justify a modest investment in testing tools in order to reduce the error rate. Alternatively, it might consider design changes that would allow real-time monitoring of the orders so that individual problems with orders could be identified and corrected before they result in a loss of revenue. With a $900,000 improvement possible, Business C could probably justify a broad strategy involving a comprehensive continuous process improvement program, real-time monitoring, and an improved testing process.

Although the loss of any given order has only a small impact on the online ordering businesses, such is not the case for the construction business. Failing to produce a result in this business means defaulting on a $33,000,000 contract and could well mean the end of the business. In such businesses, the real-time monitoring approach is really the only viable option. You can observe this if you examine a typical con-

Table 12–5: *Impact of Processing Failures on Online Order Businesses*

	Annual Revenue Impact		
Chance of Failure in Process	*Business A*	*Business B*	*Business C*
1.00%	$10,000	$100,000	$1,000,000
0.10%	$1,000	$10,000	$100,000
0.01%	$100	$1,000	$10,000

struction business. A substantial portion of the business operation is typically devoted to the management of each project: creating and reviewing plans, tracking the execution of the project, and dealing with deviations as they arise. Note that risk mitigation in this case is not an add-on to the business process—the core business process is the active management of the project itself! Here an understanding of the risks results in very fundamental changes to the business process, making the active management of risk a fundamental part of the process.

Multiple Failure Modes

Things get more complicated when a single process produces multiple results, as there are additional failure modes in which the process produces one of the results but not the other. For example, in the online retail business, there is more to the process than just shipping the goods. You need to get paid as well. So the overall order-to-cash business process for these businesses involves two results: the shipment of the goods and the receipt of the payment. Such situations lead to additional types of failures: shipping the goods and not getting paid, or getting paid and not shipping the goods. Each of these failure modes has different risks—which are sometimes very different—as the next example demonstrates.

Consider the business process used to sell lottery tickets. The process produces three results: the ticket itself, the receipt of payment, and a record of the wager. For the moment, ignore the payment and concentrate on the ticket and the record. One of the possible failure modes results in the generation of a lottery ticket but no record of the wager. Another results in the record of the wager but no lottery ticket.

The difference in consequences for these two failure cases is startling. The actual business you are considering operates lotteries on a contract basis. For this business, the consequences of failing to print the ticket are small: an annoyed customer and the loss of revenue from the sale of a single ticket. While being far from desirable, such failures are not catastrophic on a per-incident basis.

In contrast, the consequences of failing to keep a record of the wager are vastly different. Without the record of the wager, the enterprise does not have the ability to either validate the lottery ticket or determine how many winning tickets there actually are. Without knowing how many winning tickets there are, the amount to be paid to each winner cannot be determined. On top of that, not having a record of the ticket makes the enterprise vulnerable to fraud as it has no means of validating a winning ticket.

So what is the potential cost to the enterprise that results from failing to keep a record of the wager? You might be tempted to say that the cost is something like the value of the current lottery jackpot. In actuality, the cost is much larger: It is the value of the enterprise itself! The enterprise in question operates lotteries as a service business. If an incident ever occurs in which there is a dispute over what appears to be a winning ticket, the enterprise's customers will lose faith in its ability to provide the lottery service and will go elsewhere for the service. The enterprise will go out of business.

How does this enterprise manage these risks? It designs its business process so that it is not possible to print a lottery ticket without first verifying that records of the wager have been successfully saved on multiple disks in multiple and physically separated computing centers. The lottery ticket cannot be printed until these recordings have been verified. Thus only a loss of all the physically separated computing centers will yield the high-risk result. Notice that this risk reduction strategy did not involve just adding extra risk management logic or extra testing to an existing business process. The strategy required structuring the business process itself to reduce the risk. Such strategies are, of course, possible only if the risks are understood and taken into consideration at the time the business process is designed. On the other hand, such strategies tend to be less expensive, less complicated, and more reliable than add-on strategies.

The Risk of Error

Business processes are not perfect, and neither are the systems that support them. They make mistakes. Sometimes these mistakes result in the creation of an incorrect result. For example, a business process might accept an order but deliver the wrong goods. The process might ship the wrong quantity or ship to the wrong address. While in some cases you might consider such errors to be outright failures, in other cases the error results in additional costs associated with the correction of the error. In such cases, you need to understand these potential costs in order to determine how much to invest in reducing the errors.

If the wrong goods are delivered, someone has to take the call from the customer, arrange for the return and restocking of the erroneous goods, and arrange for the correct goods to be shipped. There are labor costs involved, and some of the returned goods may no longer be in saleable condition. Table 12–6 shows what the business impact might be for our online ordering companies. Note that the differences in the revenue impact are partially driven by the difference in average order sizes. The larger companies have fewer, larger orders.

Mitigating error risks generally involves the explicit evaluation of results at specific points in the business process. This provides a means of identifying that an error has occurred. Coupled with an appropriate business process response, this enables errors to be caught and corrected before they result in a final erroneous result. This risk reduction may be as simple as returning a promise (a record of the order) to the `Requestor` (the person placing the order) containing the details of what is being promised. This allows the `Requestor` to identify any errors and take action to correct them, presumably at a cost significantly lower than that of correcting an erroneous final result. In the order entry example, this feedback might be as simple as sending an e-mail detailing the items, their quantities, and the projected delivery dates.

The costs associated with different kinds of errors vary wildly. Design flaws in a construction business can be extraordinarily expensive to

Table 12–6: *Business Impact of Order Errors*

Chance of Error in Process	Per Order Cost of Error Correction	Annual Revenue Impact		
		Business A	Business B	Business C
1.00%	$40	$20,000	$80,000	$160,000
0.10%	$40	$2,000	$8,000	$16,000
0.01%	$40	$200	$800	$1,600

correct. Other errors violate regulatory constraints that have associated cost penalties. For example, financial institutions are at risk if they ignore a "Do not contact" directive from a customer. By U.S. law, if a customer has given such a directive to a financial institution, that institution is liable for a $10,000 penalty for each subsequent call made to that customer. Clearly, such cost penalties warrant risk mitigation investments.

Business costs resulting from errors can vary widely depending on the nature of the error. A 1% error rate in delivering orders might impact the bottom line by a few percentage points, whereas the same 1% error rate resulting in regulatory noncompliance might result in bankruptcy. Understanding the true business cost of errors is a necessary prerequisite to determining the appropriate level of investment to make in reducing those errors.

The Risk of Delay

The world does not always run on time, and the same is true for business processes. For some processes, such as stopping your car or trading stocks, failing to deliver the results on time is tantamount to failure. For many other business processes, lateness is not failure, but it does have costs associated with it. One consequence is that customers will perceive the tardiness as poor service and will choose to do business next time with a competitor. Exceptional performance, on the other hand, can help win customers away from the competition. Evaluating such risks and rewards obviously requires a deep understanding of the business and market conditions. Clearly, this is an area in which the business side of the house must make a determination as to the level of investment it wishes to make.

Lateness can have other penalties as well. In business-to-business interactions, there are often explicit financial penalties. Table 12–7 shows the statistical impact of a 20% late delivery penalty on our online ordering businesses.

You need to look at delay costs on a per-incident basis as well. While the per-incident cost in our ordering businesses is small ($4 to $50), in the construction business, a 20% late fee for a $33,000,000 job is a whopping $6,600,00 penalty! Clearly, some action is warranted here to ensure that the project is completed on time!

Table 12–7: *Business Cost of Late Delivery for Orders*

Chance of Late Delivery	Penalty for Late Delivery	Annual Revenue Impact		
		Business A	Business B	Business C
10.00%	20.00%	$20,000	$200,000	$2,000,000
1.00%	20.00%	$2,000	$20,000	$200,000
0.10%	20.00%	$200	$2,000	$20,000

Lateness is typically mitigated by monitoring the process. These monitoring results can be used in two complementary ways. One is to guide a continuous process improvement effort in which the monitoring results are used to identify the sources of lateness. The ensuing investigation results in a process improvement that reduces the likelihood of future incidents. The other use of the monitoring results is to identify and correct individual jobs that are falling behind schedule. In extreme cases, such as the construction business, this monitoring itself becomes the very core of the business process.

Summary

Business processes and systems exist to produce results. When those results are not produced or are in error or late, there are consequences for the business. These consequences vary widely depending on both the type of breakdown and the nature of the business. Each type of breakdown presents a different type of risk to the enterprise. Errors that might lead to a small profit reduction in one business might lead to bankruptcy in another. You must understand the specific consequences of breakdowns in your business in order to understand which types of breakdowns warrant your attention.

Investments can be made that will mitigate the risks associated with breakdowns. But each type of breakdown requires a different type of investment to reduce that particular type of risk. In order to decide which investments are warranted, you must understand the consequences of each type of breakdown. Only then will it be clear which types of breakdowns warrant an investment in process and systems design, and what level of investment should be considered.

Incorporating this understanding into your business process and systems design process is, in most enterprises, a fundamental change in the design process. This entire chapter essentially argues that you must include an understanding of the business situation and associated risks and let this understanding guide design decisions! This understanding will impact the design patterns you choose for the business process and underlying system. It will impact the kind of task management dialogs you employ and your decision as to whether or not fault tolerance or high availability is warranted. It will impact the level of testing and the investment in testing tools that are warranted.

The bottom line is that selecting appropriate risk mitigation and management strategies and levels of investment requires an understanding of the business risks involved. These selections are not technology decisions, nor are they decisions that can be made based on abstract principles. Appropriate investments in risk reduction can be made only with the full understanding of the business consequences. Although the project team executes these decisions, the business responsibility for the decisions and the business risk lies with the business executive sponsor.

Key Business Process Risk Reduction Questions

Disruptions in a single business process execution:

1. What business consequences arise from a single execution of the business process failing to produce the required result? What level of investment is warranted in avoiding such individual failures?

2. What business consequences arise from a single execution of the business process producing an erroneous result? What level of investment is warranted in avoiding individual errors?

3. What business consequences arise from a late delivery of a single result? What level of investment is warranted in avoiding this occurrence?

Disruptions affecting multiple executions of the business process:

1. What business consequences arise from the business process being unavailable for some period of time? What level of investment is warranted in improving process availability?

2. What business consequences arise from a loss of all work in progress in the business process? What level of investment is warranted in avoiding this loss?

3. What business consequences arise from a percentage of business process executions failing to produce their required results? What level of investment is warranted in reducing this percentage?

4. What business consequences arise from a percentage of business process executions producing erroneous results? What level of investment is warranted in reducing this percentage?

5. What business consequences arise from a percentage of business process executions producing late results? What level of investment is warranted in reducing this percentage?

Chapter 13

Managing SOA Risks

Adding SOA to your world means adding risks. Services have a definite upside, but there are new categories of risks involved as well. One category relates to the usability of the service. Going back to return on investment, you won't get the ROI you want unless the service interface represents a point of stability in the overall enterprise architecture. Thus, the service really has to be well suited for its purpose.

Service-Related Risks

Being well suited is not a black-and-white thing for a service but rather a grey-scale spectrum. At one extreme, the service either provides functionality that isn't needed at all or provides its functionality in a manner that doesn't support the real business need. This typically occurs as a result of purely speculative development. In this case, developers simply don't take the time to research and understand what functionality is actually needed. The consequence is that the entire investment in the service is wasted. You can mitigate this risk by requiring a justification for every service, a justification that not only demonstrates the need for the service but also includes an analysis of those usages.

A more common risk is that a service is built to satisfy only one usage. This is typical of a service being developed specifically as part of a project that will use the service. That project's use of the service is well understood, but potential future usages of the service are not investigated. One consequence is that modifications will likely be required to support future usages, and these changes erode, if not eliminate, the anticipated ROI. A common cause of this problem is a view that every interface ought to be a service operation. Such policies increase IT costs and yield no benefit. Again, requiring a service justification will mitigate this risk.

Another risk is that applicable services won't get used, even though they are available and appropriate. Two factors contribute to this situation. One is a breakdown in communications: The advertising of available services is inadequate, or the indexing and documentation associated with the service are insufficient to support the identification of appropriate services. You can mitigate this risk by putting in place a well-organized and well-indexed directory of services.

The other factor that contributes to the nonuse of services is the "not invented here" syndrome. Finding an existing service and learning enough about it to use it effectively requires real work. If the developers believe it will be less work to rebuild the functionality than to learn about the existing service, they are likely not to use the service. You can mitigate this risk by reviewing the use of services in the project's architecture prior to implementation.

You should note that the quality of the advertising, indexing, and documenting of services has as much impact on service usage as the developers' attitudes. Also note, however, that creating these artifacts actually drives up the cost of creating services, making it all the more important that you justify the service.

Another risk is that changing business circumstances end up changing the requirements for the service. Adding a new product distribution channel, for example, might require significant changes to the processes by which products are packaged and shipped. This, in turn, will impact the services that manage orders and shipments. To some extent, this risk is unavoidable. However, you can mitigate this risk by involving senior personnel in the justification and specification of services. For infrastructure services, these are the senior IT architects who are cognizant of the trends in technology and design practices. For business services, these are the senior business process architects and planners who are aware of corporate and market trends.

Partial implementation of a service can also present a risk. The initial implementation of a service often focuses on the creation and modification of things—orders, for example—and neglects the operations for marking things obsolete or purging old information. The consequence is that implementing these operations at a later time may require extensive modification of the earlier service implementation and may even require changes to the existing interfaces, both of which drive up costs. You can mitigate this risk by requiring that the initial service design include the entire lifecycle for each entity managed by the service: create, read, update, and delete (often referred to as the CRUD cycle). The operations do not necessarily have to be implemented, but by designing them you reduce the cost of their eventual implementation.

SOA Processes and Governance

Governance is the process of risk management. Knowing how to mitigate a risk does not lessen the risk. You have to actually execute the mitigation strategy in order to reduce risk. The governance processes you put into place determine the points at which you will assess risk and confirm that the appropriate mitigation strategies have been employed.

There are four major processes associated with SOA, each of which requires governance: project portfolio planning, service design, service utilization, and service operation. But before you can define the governance, you have to define the process being governed. Thus, establishing governance also standardizes these processes.

The actual processes you use for each of these tasks will vary greatly from enterprise to enterprise. These variations are driven by both cultural and organizational differences and result primarily in differences in the level of formality, the number and content of the artifacts generated in the process, and the number and intent of the governance checkpoints in each process.

Despite these variations, successful SOA processes all exhibit some common features. They share some common milestones, governance points at which SOA risks are evaluated and mitigated. Let's look at these processes and their governance points.

Governance for Project Portfolio Planning

Most enterprises already have some form of project portfolio planning. In this process, ideas for new projects are evaluated and prioritized. Budgetary estimates (not to be confused with engineering estimates) are prepared to outline the anticipated project cost and time to complete. Finally, these proposals are compared against the available budget, and a certain number of projects are funded. Depending on the organization and how budgets are allocated, this may be a singular centralized activity or a series of planning activities, one for each IT organization holding a development budget.

In order to be successful with services, you have to extend this planning activity a bit. Recognizing that you won't get an ROI from the first use of a service, it is prudent for you to think about the portfolio of projects in terms of which ones will create services and which ones will be consumers of services. This obviously creates dependencies between projects that impact the sequence in which the projects will be executed. It may also influence your thinking about project priorities. If a major project requires a service that does not yet exist, the creation of that service must become part of the portfolio plan, whether it is in that project or another.

There is a measure of speculation in this exercise, speculation about what is important to the business, about what you think the project costs and schedule will be, and about what services will be created and used. Because of the speculation involved, you have to expect that the unfolding of reality will render some of these speculations inaccurate. Changing business conditions will alter priorities. In-progress projects will discover that the budgetary estimates are inaccurate. The act of justifying or attempting to use a service will alter your thinking about what services are appropriate.

The typical project portfolio planning process has an annual cycle that is synchronized with the fiscal calendar of the enterprise. At a minimum, you need to integrate services planning into this annual process. You need to add an activity for developing a cross-project services plan and a governance step for reviewing this plan before the project portfolio is finalized.

In addition to this annual exercise, it is prudent to add quarterly or semiannual checkpoints. This governance step compares the actual project progress against the plan and determines whether adjustments to the project portfolio are warranted. This governance review must evaluate progress against the services plan as well as cost and schedule progress.

Governance for Service Design

Deciding to build a service is an investment decision and should be treated as such. Implementing functionality as a service always requires more work than a basic implementation of the functionality. The service, by itself, provides no value. Its value lies in its use, and its return on investment relies on its continued use in the light of business process and systems changes. The decision to build a service thus requires weighing the savings to be derived through continued use (i.e., avoiding subsequent modifications) against the incremental cost of converting the functionality into a service.

Governance: Balancing Education and Enforcement

Governance is the process of making sure that things are being done the way they are supposed to be done. Governance generally employs two techniques: education and enforcement. The point of education is to ensure that what needs to be done is done right the first time. The point of enforcement is to catch mistakes before they become serious.

There is a tendency in services governance to rely too heavily on enforcement. An architecture review is certainly an appropriate place to catch a mistake in either the design or the use of services. Unfortunately, by that point the design team has made a significant investment in the design. While the review catches the mistake before you make any additional investment in implementation, fixing design mistakes still takes time and resources.

Education will help to avoid design mistakes. Education, however, requires investment. How to "do it right" has to be defined and documented by the SOA leadership team, and this knowledge must be transferred to the project design team through some combination of formal training, mentoring, and reading.

You will have a hard time with SOA if your entire approach to governance is enforcement. It will be like establishing a speed limit on a highway without posting signs to tell drivers what the speed limit is. For your SOA efforts to be successful, your enterprise-specific vision of SOA and your enterprise-specific best practices for achieving that vision must be captured and shared.

The governance of service creation centers around the following three points:

1. Ensuring that the creation of the service is appropriately justified and specified
2. Ensuring that the service is implemented appropriately
3. Ensuring that the service development process produces the artifacts required to support its future usages

The details of precisely where these governance activities will fit within your development processes will vary greatly depending on your development practices and organizations. The following sections define what needs to be done and when it needs to be done. It is up to you to determine the details and ensure that it actually happens!

Service Justification and Specification

Justifying a service means making a determination that the additional cost involved in implementing functionality as a service is justified by anticipated future cost avoidance. Cost is avoided either by having a new client reuse the existing service or by having a service interface that remains stable when the service implementation changes in the future.

Specifying a service means defining it so that it will support the anticipated future usages without further modification. Accomplishing this requires a due-diligence analysis of these anticipated usages—a bit of crystal ball gazing.

There are two challenges in service justification and specification. One lies in simply ensuring that these tasks are performed. The other lies in making sure that the right people are involved in the process.

While some projects may be chartered exclusively to build new services, these are by far the exception. You generally charter such service-building projects only at the beginning of an enterprise's services initiative. Their focus lies in getting an initial set of infrastructure services in place to support the building of business services.

The ideas for business services, on the other hand, tend to arise in ordinary projects. The project team recognizes that a particular set of functionality might make sense as a service. The problem that these project teams generally face is that the only usage of the proposed service that they are intimately familiar with is the one associated with the present project. This narrow perspective presents a problem. In order to determine whether a service makes sense, other potential uses need to be examined. Who will do this exploration? More importantly, who has the proper perspective to do this exploration?

Getting the right people involved in justification and specification is the biggest challenge in business services. The people you want to involve are the most experienced architects and planners in your organization—people who already know the present landscape and future directions of the enterprise and can determine whether the service will fit. These are the senior systems architects for infrastructure services and the senior business process architects and business planners for business services. Most of the time, these people are not actively involved in the current project. You need a procedure to get them involved, and you need to make their responses to the request a priority.

For efficiency, this involvement of the senior architects and planners should be structured into two distinct tasks: justification and specification. Justification should focus on weeding out the proposals that don't make sense as services. While justification must explore the different potential usages, it does not have to detail them. When justification concludes that a service does make sense, then a deeper exploration of these usages is required so that the service and its operations can be fully specified. Once the architects have completed the specification, then responsibility for the implementation of the service can revert back to the project team. Governance of service justification and specification requires the following:

1. A procedure to get the appropriate senior architects involved in evaluating and specifying proposed services
2. Prioritization of the senior architects' time to ensure that they respond to evaluation and specification requests in a timely manner
3. Well-defined criteria for evaluating service proposals (discussed in Chapter 4) and specifying services (discussed in this book's companion volume, *SOA in Practice: Implementing Total Architecture*)
4. A checklist item in the project's architecture review to ensure that proposed new services have been appropriately justified

Service Architecture, Implementation, and Deployment

On the surface, building a service very much resembles the development of any other component or application. The service specification defines the basic requirements, with additional requirements arising from enterprise best practices regarding the design and operation of services.

But the operation of other components depends on the proper operation of services. Consequently, you expect more stability from services than you would ordinarily expect from other components. In particular, the supported components rely on the service providing its specified functionality while meeting all performance goals and providing the specified level of reliability.

These expectations place increased demands on the implementation process in two areas: architecture and testing. In architecture, you have to ensure that the proposed design is capable of providing the full range of specified functionality while meeting performance and reliability/availability goals. While the same might be said of other components, you have to keep in mind that you are building services to save time and money. Design and implementation errors uncovered in future usages will require revisions that will likely eat up the anticipated cost savings that justified the service in the first place.

Performance and capacity require particularly close attention in service architecture and design. The obvious aspect of this is ensuring that the design is capable of providing the specified performance when loaded to its planned capacity. Perhaps not as obvious is the need to design into the service the ability to measure and report the actual demands being placed on it while it is in use. These measurements will enable you to determine when these demands are beginning to approach the design limits and therefore will help you to anticipate the need to deploy additional capacity.

Another challenge to the service architecture is scalability. The anticipated future usage of the service may call for capacity well beyond the initial demand—so far beyond that it is not cost-effective to initially deploy the full service capacity. In such cases, it is prudent to design the service in such a way that capacity can be incrementally added as new service users come online. Documentation must be provided to describe the manner in which capacity can be incrementally added. This documentation should include instructions for calculating the resources required to support different demand levels.

Testing the implementation's compliance with its specification is another area warranting special attention. Isolating problems to a particular service in a SOA is a particularly tedious and time-consuming task. Thorough testing of the service prior to its integration into the overall SOA will cost less than discovering and fixing problems after integration. Furthermore, finding and correcting problems in the service after its initial deployment will erode, if not eliminate, the cost savings that justified the creation of the service in the first place. Governance of service implementation requires two things.

1. A thorough architectural review to ensure that the proposed service design will satisfy its requirements. This type of review is an important milestone in the development of any component or service.

2. Comprehensive testing to ensure functional and nonfunctional compliance with specifications. A checklist item should be added to the predeployment review to ensure that the testing has been adequate.

Service Documentation

Services should be designed specifically to support future usage. Because of this, an investment must be made in providing enough information to support those future usages and in placing that information in the appropriate places.

The required information must span an entire spectrum of inquiry from a simple "What is it?" to a detailed "Is it capable of performing the xyz operation at a rate of 273 transactions/second with a 0.5-second response time on a 24×7 basis with 99.9% availability?" At a minimum, documenting a service requires the following.

1. A one-line functional description of the service. This is essential for quickly determining whether a given service even addresses the functional area of interest. The act of creating a one-line description is often a good litmus test to determine whether a service is well conceived. The need to add amplifying information may indicate that the service covers only a fragment of a functional area or that it includes fragments belonging to other functional areas.

2. An abstract of the service outlining its intended purpose and important constraints. The abstract provides another level of detail and is intended to support efficient weeding out of inappropriate services. The abstract should be a one-paragraph description of the service that augments the one-line description with information about its intended use. Important performance or reliability capabilities or limitations should be mentioned.

3. A comprehensive description of the service. This is the user's guide to the service. It should contain the full service specifications, augmented with explanatory material that fully characterizes the intended use of the service. The documentation should include examples of using the service and instructions as to how to prepare an application for using this particular service.

4. A formal specification of the service interfaces. If you are using SOAP, this is the WSDL (web-services description language) description of the service.

Your enterprise will likely develop its own repositories for service-related information, and some (or all) of it may end up in a UDDI (universal description, discovery, and integration) registry. But documentation, by itself, has no value. People need to be able to find and use the documentation efficiently. Whatever your strategy for disseminating information about your services, you must ensure that the documentation for each service finds its way into your service advertising, repositories, registries, and indexes. Governance of service documentation requires the following:

1. A work thread in the implementation project to generate the required documentation

2. A checklist item in the predeployment review to ensure that the required documentation has been created and deployed into the appropriate registries and repositories and has been indexed appropriately

Governance for Service Utilization

The existence of a service does not, in and of itself, provide any value. It is the use of the service that provides value and the second and subsequent uses of the service that provide the return on the services investment. Thus, you must pay attention to service utilization in order to actually get your ROI.

The most convenient way to ensure service utilization is to integrate its governance with the normal project governance. There are two key places in the project lifecycle at which service utilization should be considered: the architecture review and the predeployment review.

The architecture review is the appropriate place to determine whether services are being used appropriately. The reviewers (business process and systems architects) should consider, as part of the architecture review, whether existing services have been appropriately employed and whether new services have been appropriately justified and specified (see the previous section, Governance for Service Design). The reviewers should also consider whether other functionality ought to be evaluated as a potential service.

However, as we mentioned in the sidebar on balancing education and enforcement, it is prudent for the project team to educate itself, prior to the architecture review, about existing services and the processes for creating new services. This will lead to a more efficient development process, as it will avoid redesign after the architecture review to better align the project with the enterprise's service strategy.

The predeployment review for the project is the best place to determine whether the appropriate planning has been done for using existing services. Has the organization responsible for each service been engaged to determine whether the service has the capacity required to support the intended utilization? Are there appropriate plans in place for granting access to the production version of the service and establishing access rights?

Service utilization governance requires three things.

1. Project team education regarding the enterprise's SOA strategy and the practices for finding and using existing services.

2. A checklist item in the project's architecture review to ensure the appropriate use of services in the project. This review must occur prior to any significant development work to minimize the cost impact of changes arising from the review.

3. A checklist item in the predeployment review to ensure that existing services have been prepared for their planned utilization.

Governance for Service Operation

Services typically require operational support after their deployment, and the responsibility for this support must be clearly assigned. These support responsibilities cover three broad areas: performance monitoring, new usage planning, and upgrade planning.

Successful services will have many other components depending on their proper operation. Service monitoring is required to ensure proper operation. Service performance must be measured to ensure that the service is meeting its service-level agreements. Service utilization levels must also be measured and compared against current deployed capacity. When demand begins to approach these limits, you must deploy additional system resources. This comparison must project far enough into the future to account for the time it will take to acquire the additional resources needed to increase capacity.

Another operational responsibility is new usage governance. Several activities are required when new projects want to use existing services. One of these is to ensure that the new usage is appropriate for the service. Another is to do the capacity planning associated with the increased demand that will result. A third is managing the actual access to the service. These governance activities are essential for services. Unplanned service utilization can have an adverse effect on service performance and a corresponding adverse impact on the other service clients.

The third operational responsibility is planning and coordinating service outages and upgrades. Since a service outage will impact service clients, such outages need to be carefully planned and coordinated. You must similarly plan the deployment of new versions. Although the preferred deployment of a new version puts it into service alongside the older version, the eventual migration of all the clients to the new service must be planned and executed before the old version can be retired.

Service operational governance requires the following:

1. An organizational assignment of operational responsibility for each service
2. Operational monitoring of service performance and evaluation of performance measurements
3. A procedure for adding new service users
4. Procedures for planning service outages
5. Procedures for planning service version upgrades

Summary

Services have a lot of potential for providing benefit to the enterprise, but their use brings a level of risk as well. Some of these risks are financial, while others are operational. All can be satisfactorily mitigated through appropriate governance activities.

The biggest financial risks revolve around getting services used. It always costs more to build a service than it does to just implement the functionality in a conventional manner. This additional cost is recovered by avoiding subsequent development, through either the reuse of the service or the isolation of service clients from internal service implementation changes.

Governance is required to manage these financial risks. Governance ensures that services are not built unless they are warranted and that services are used wherever they should be. These governance activities break down into four broad areas.

Project portfolio governance coordinates the creation of services in one project with their use in other projects. Beyond the technical planning of who will use what services, this planning actually coordinates the investment (the creation of the service) with the ROI (the second and subsequent use of the service).

Service design governance ensures that each service actually makes sense. It explores the potential uses of the service and makes sure that they are similar enough that a common service will provide benefit. It goes on to detail the specification of the service to ensure its utility in all of these situations.

Project governance ensures that projects use (and create) services where appropriate. It also ensures that the appropriate capacity planning and access control have been done for services already in existence.

Operational governance ensures that someone keeps an eye on the service after it has been placed into operation. It makes sure that the service is operating properly, increasing capacity as demand requires. It coordinates new usages, again increasing capacity as required. Finally, it coordinates the operation of the service with service clients and the upgrade to new service versions when required.

Key SOA Risk Reduction Questions

1. What is the plan for creating services in your enterprise? How is this plan related to individual projects?

2. Who coordinates the creation of services and their subsequent use when these activities occur in different projects?

3. What is the process by which services are justified and specified? When do these activities occur?

4. How do you ensure that your existing services are appropriately used in new projects?

5. How do you manage new users for existing services? Who does the capacity planning and access control?

6. How do you manage the operation of your services? Who coordinates their planned outages with the service clients?

7. How do you manage service version upgrades? Who coordinates the upgrades of the service clients?

Afterword

This book has covered a lot of ground. It has covered how business processes and projects can go wrong, as well as various ways to keep things on track. It's time to tie it all together and consider where to go from here. Let's start with a recap of major ideas.

1. *Define success*: When you charter a project, you need to paint a clear picture of what the project needs to accomplish. Quantifying the expected benefits and making the measurement of those benefits one of the project requirements keeps the project focused on achieving these benefits.

2. *Quantify risks*: Business process failures entail risk for the enterprise, and mitigating these risks requires investment. Different business processes entail different levels of risk and thus warrant different levels of investment. In order for the project to make wise investments in risk reduction, the project leadership team needs a quantitative understanding of these risks.

3. *Pay attention to operations*: Computers are limited in their flexibility, so you need people to respond flexibly to the unexpected. In order to keep your business processes flowing smoothly, systems must alert operations personnel when the unexpected occurs, and those personnel must respond in a timely manner. You need to make sure that the operations personnel are organized and have the processes in place to ensure a timely response.

4. *Assign end-to-end responsibility*: Make sure that the project manager is focused on providing the expected business benefit and that the business process and systems architects are looking at the end-to-end business processes and systems. Their collective responsibility is to see that the business processes and systems actually produce the expected business benefits.

5. *Make architecture explicit*: Insist that development projects include an explicit architecture step that encompasses both business process and systems design. This architecture describes how the business

processes and systems will work together to provide the expected business benefits. It produces enough information to create an accurate cost and schedule estimate and thus makes it possible to determine whether the project can be reasonably completed within the given cost and schedule guidelines. Ensure that this architectural work is substantially complete prior to beginning any significant systems development.

6. *Demand feasibility feedback*: Insist that the project team report back as early as practicable regarding the feasibility of achieving the expected business benefits within the project's cost and schedule guidelines. Be prepared to hear that the initial cost and schedule guidelines are insufficient.

7. *Encourage iterative architecture development*: Employ an iterative methodology that explores feasibility first provides the earliest possible feedback about infeasible projects with minimal investment of time and resources. This approach minimizes business risk and helps keep resources productively focused on producing tangible business benefits.

8. *Establish a proactive enterprise architecture group* (if you don't already have one): Charter it to comprehensively cover business processes, application design, infrastructure, and data. This group ensures consistency of goals and techniques across projects and is a critical element of a service-oriented architecture effort. Make sure that the enterprise architecture group is actively involved in guiding and governing every project that spans multiple business units.

9. *Provide active management support*: The enterprise architecture group and all projects involving multiple business units require active management support. This support is needed to ensure that business unit priorities are aligned with project and enterprise architecture goals. For each project, identify the business executive sponsor responsible for business unit cooperation and the IT executive sponsor responsible for IT unit cooperation. Do the same for the enterprise architecture group.

Next Steps: The Enterprise Architecture Roadmap

The ideas in this book will not benefit your enterprise until you put them into practice. To benefit from these ideas, you need to compare and contrast them with your current practices. You can use the questions at the end of each chapter to perform a gap analysis and identify those areas in which your enterprise needs improvement.

The next step is to determine how you will close the gaps. You must blend the ideas of this book with your organization's current practices and determine how you want your enterprise to develop business processes and systems in the future. The result of this exercise should be an enterprise roadmap that covers the following topics.

1. *Enterprise architecture vision*: Create a shareable document that describes the future-state enterprise architecture and the business rationale behind the vision. This document clearly articulates the business value expected from the enterprise architecture in a manner that is accessible to both business and IT personnel.

2. *Enterprise architecture organization*: Describe how the enterprise architecture group will be organized and to whom it will report. Describe how this group will coordinate all aspects of total architecture (i.e., business processes, applications, data, and infrastructure). Describe how enterprise architecture priorities will be brought into alignment with individual business unit priorities.

3. *Project organization*: Describe how projects involving multiple business units will be organized and to whom they will report. Describe how business unit priorities will be brought into alignment with the enterprise priorities as reflected in the project charter.

4. *Project oversight and governance*: Describe the development process that enterprise projects will follow and the related milestones, deliverables, and governance checkpoints. Describe how project feasibility will be established. Describe how the alignment of the project's architecture with the enterprise architecture will be validated. Describe how the discovery, creation, and use of services will be managed.

5. *Architecture skills*: Describe how the needed architecture skills will be provided for each project. Describe how architects will be trained and how projects will be staffed with architects. Describe the conditions under which enterprise architects should directly participate in the formulation of the project architecture. Identify the related organizational responsibilities.

6. *Infrastructure*: Describe the systems infrastructure that must be put in place to support the enterprise architecture vision. Provide a timetable for putting this infrastructure in place, and define who will be responsible for the operation and maintenance of the infrastructure.

7. *Operational processes*: Describe the processes to be used for operating deployed business processes, applications, and services. Describe how business process breakdowns (e.g., a problem with an order) will be detected and resolved. Describe the process for prioritizing issues, assigning responsibility for their resolution, and tracking their resolution.

8. *Training and best practices*: Describe how best practices will be established, documented, archived, and disseminated. Describe the mechanisms that will be used to transfer this knowledge to the people who require it: documentation, formal training, and direct mentoring by experts. Identify the related organizational responsibilities.

9. *Roadmap maintenance*: Describe the process that will be used to refresh the roadmap and keep it consistent with changing business conditions and evolving technologies. Specify how often this maintenance will occur and the related organizational responsibilities.

The roadmap represents a forward-looking view of how to get things done. However, you have to recognize that some of the elements of this roadmap are untried and are likely to require refinement as they are put into practice. You need to pay careful attention to how well each element seems to be working the first time you execute it. Processes, in particular, require close attention. They need to be effective but not onerous. You want to pay particular attention to the amount of work your processes require that does not contribute directly to the expected result; keep this extraneous work to a minimum. You have to be open to feedback from participants in the processes and willing to refine and adjust the processes as you go along.

Looking to the Future

The world around you is constantly changing, creating both pressures and opportunities for your enterprise. As you examine these pressures and opportunities, you have to look for trends and understand how your enterprise must respond to these trends. Three of these trends cause the scope and complexity of your total architecture to continually expand. These trends are beginning to make the active management of your total architecture a mandatory survival tactic.

Mobile Computing

The first of these trends is a steady increase in both network capacity and mobile connectivity. This makes it easier and easier to provide and capture information at the specific location where it makes the most sense in your business processes. What you can expect from this trend is a rising use of mobile devices. As the bandwidth increases and these devices continue to grow in their power and capability, you will see more and more of these devices becoming participants in your business processes. This will add to the number of system components involved in your business processes and to the number of development groups involved in your distributed process designs. The more components and development groups you add, the more important it becomes to explicitly design the total architecture of the business processes and systems involved.

Geographic Distribution

The second trend you face is the increasing geographic distribution of both your enterprise and your development efforts. As your enterprise grows in scope, your business processes involve participants in more locations. As development goes global and you embrace outsourcing as a strategy, your development processes involve participants in multiple locations as well. This geographic distribution makes communications between the multiple business groups and multiple development groups increasingly difficult.

Studies have shown that as companies move people further apart, the likelihood of meaningful technical communications between them decreases drastically as the square of the distance between them.[1] Double the distance, and the technical communications drop by a factor of four. Put people on a different floor, and they might as well be in a different building. Put them in a different building, and they might as well be in a different city.

Distance presents an enormous obstacle to the development of distributed business processes and systems. It makes a design-by-committee approach virtually impossible in all but the most trivial cases. The only

---

1. T. J. Allen, "Architecture and Communication among Product Development Engineers," *Proceedings of the 2000 IEEE Engineering Management Society* (2000), pp. 153–158.

practical solution is to centralize the architecture of the overall business processes and systems—the total architecture. Defining the total architecture clearly delineates the responsibilities of the various business units and development groups. Only this type of explicit design will give you the confidence that the development work being done at the various sites, and the business responsibilities delegated to the various business units, will blend together into a coherent whole. Only then can you have the confidence that the resulting business process will execute properly and deliver the expected business benefits.

Service-Oriented Architectures

The third trend is the increasing use of services as a means of providing external access to the enterprise. The operations of these services provide the building blocks for assembling large-scale business processes, processes in which the enterprise as a whole is but one participant among many. You can see examples of this today in business-to-business processes involving supply chains and healthcare provisioning. You do not have to look very far down the line to imagine the day when a generic consumer application will be able to use industry-standard service interfaces to access any company's catalogs and place orders for its products.

However, in order to develop these industry-wide service standards, you need to first define the business process they are intended to support. From these abstracted business processes, you can derive the protocols by which the participants will interact. From the protocols, you can define the services and operations required to support the protocols. These abstract business processes and their supporting protocols and services are mutually interdependent. Once again, you will find total architecture at the core.

Tuning Your Enterprise Engine

Business processes and systems comprise the engine that makes the enterprise run. If you want this engine to work correctly and efficiently, you need to design it, tune it, monitor it, and manage it. If you do this effectively, your enterprise will thrive and prosper. If you do not, it will wither and die.

Total architecture is simply the design of the enterprise engine. As enterprises grow in scope and complexity and systems become more deeply embedded in business processes, the complexity of this design increases correspondingly. Traditional ad hoc piecemeal approaches to the design of the overall engine are inadequate. If you want to keep your engine not only functioning but also strongly directed toward achieving your enterprise business objectives, you must organize your enterprise to manage this engine and its design.

Managing the design of the engine is the responsibility of the business process and systems architects. At both the project and enterprise levels, architects are the stewards of the engine design. In this volume, I have talked about the need for their work and the environment required to make it successful. In *SOA in Practice: Implementing Total Architecture*, I will go on to detail the things that these architects need to do to carry out this responsibility. Collectively, these two volumes provide the knowledge you need to manage your enterprise's total architecture.

However, knowledge by itself will not improve your enterprise. You must take this knowledge and apply it. You must charter your architects to manage your total architecture and empower them to carry out this responsibility. You must establish a working environment that keeps business unit priorities aligned with overall enterprise goals. If you do these things, your enterprise engine will remain efficiently focused on producing the business value you expect from your enterprise. If you do not, your enterprise engine will deteriorate and become disconnected from its business purpose. The choice is yours.

Index

informIT

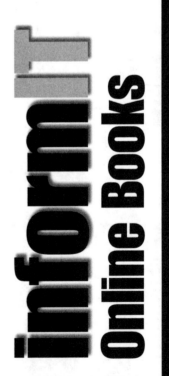